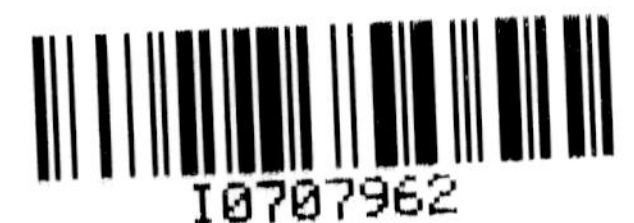

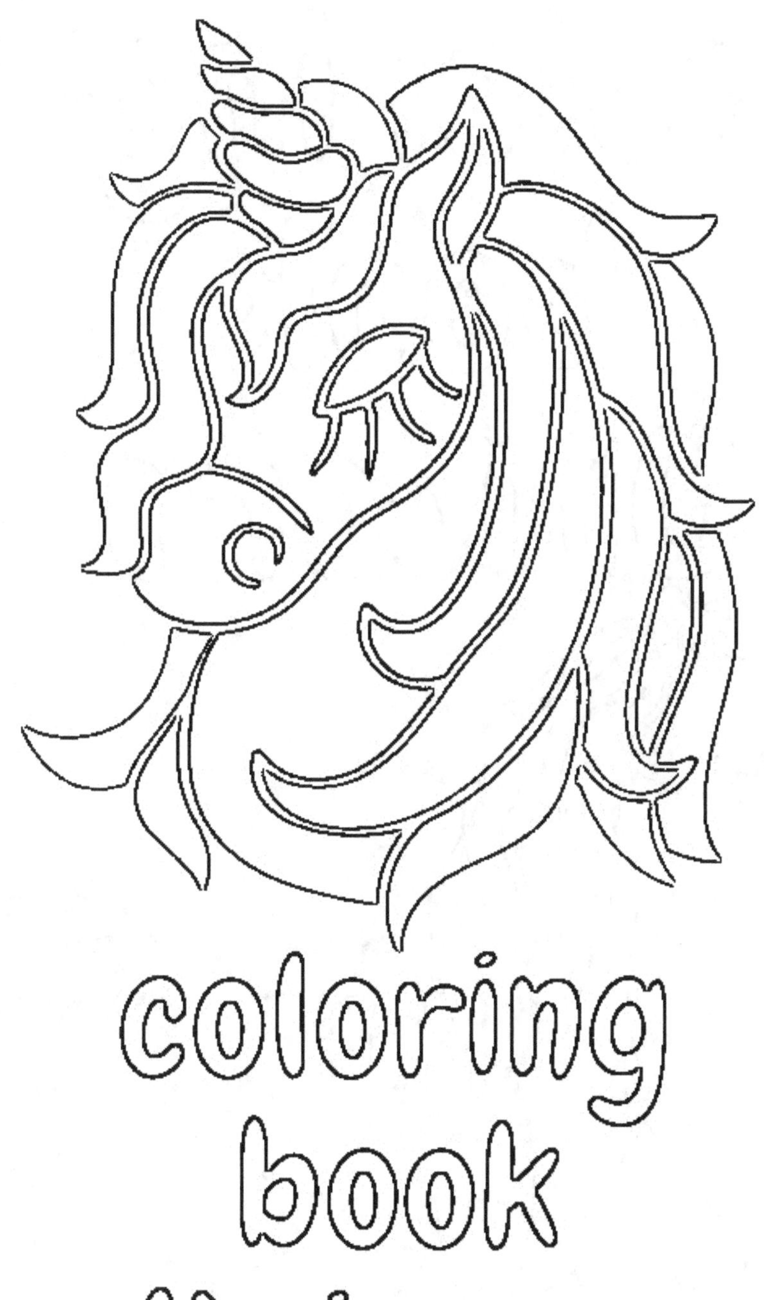

coloring book Unicorn

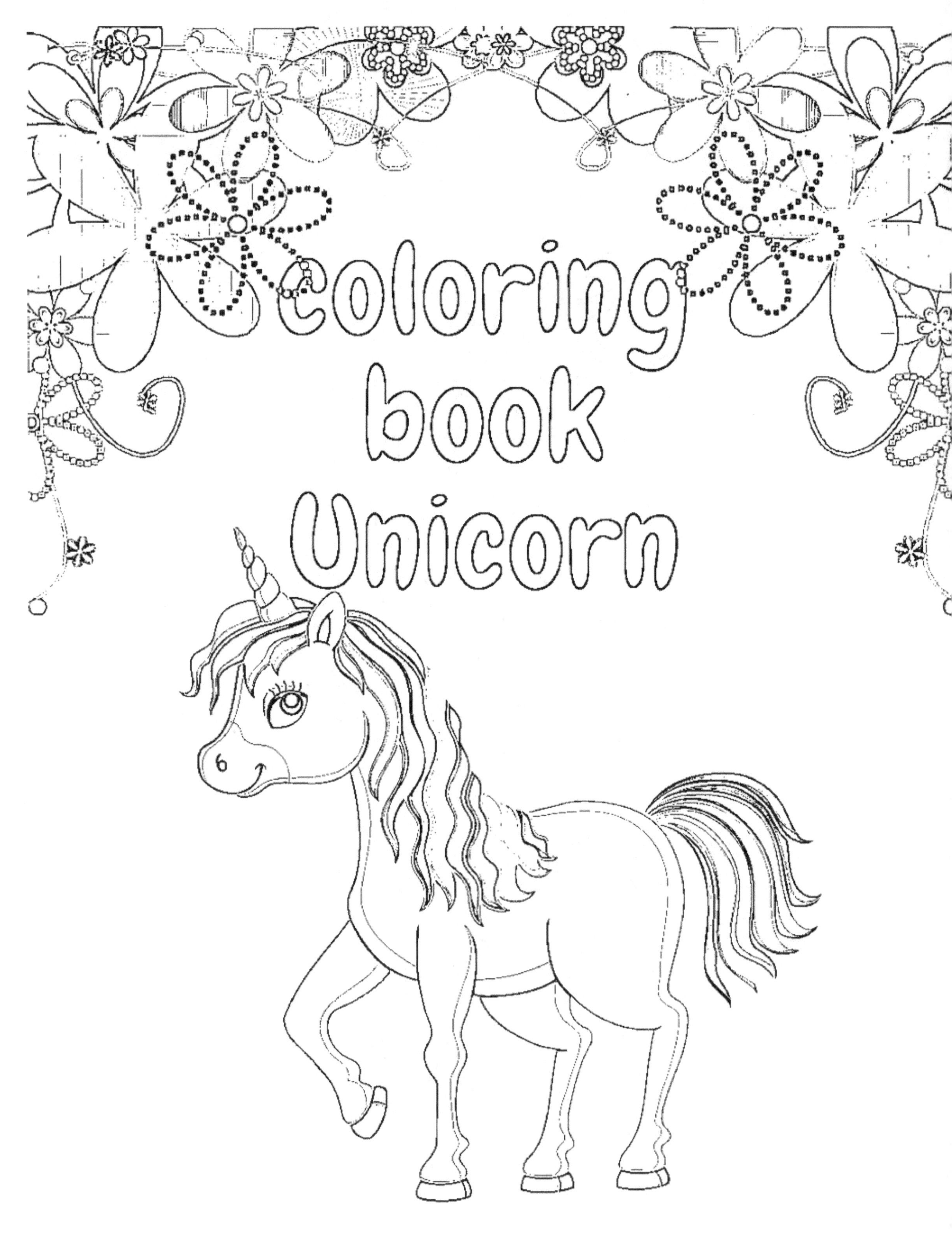
coloring
book
Unicorn

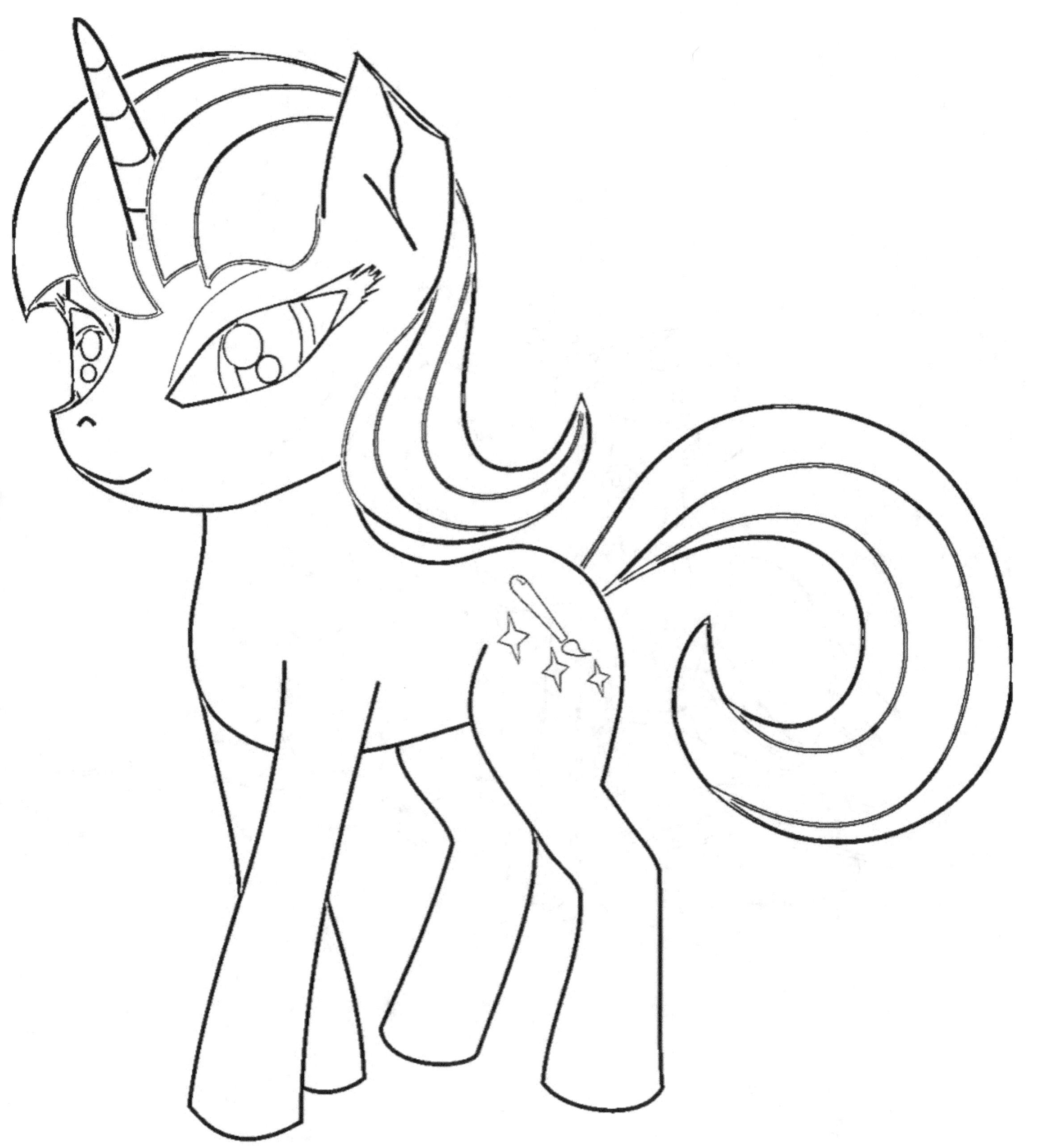

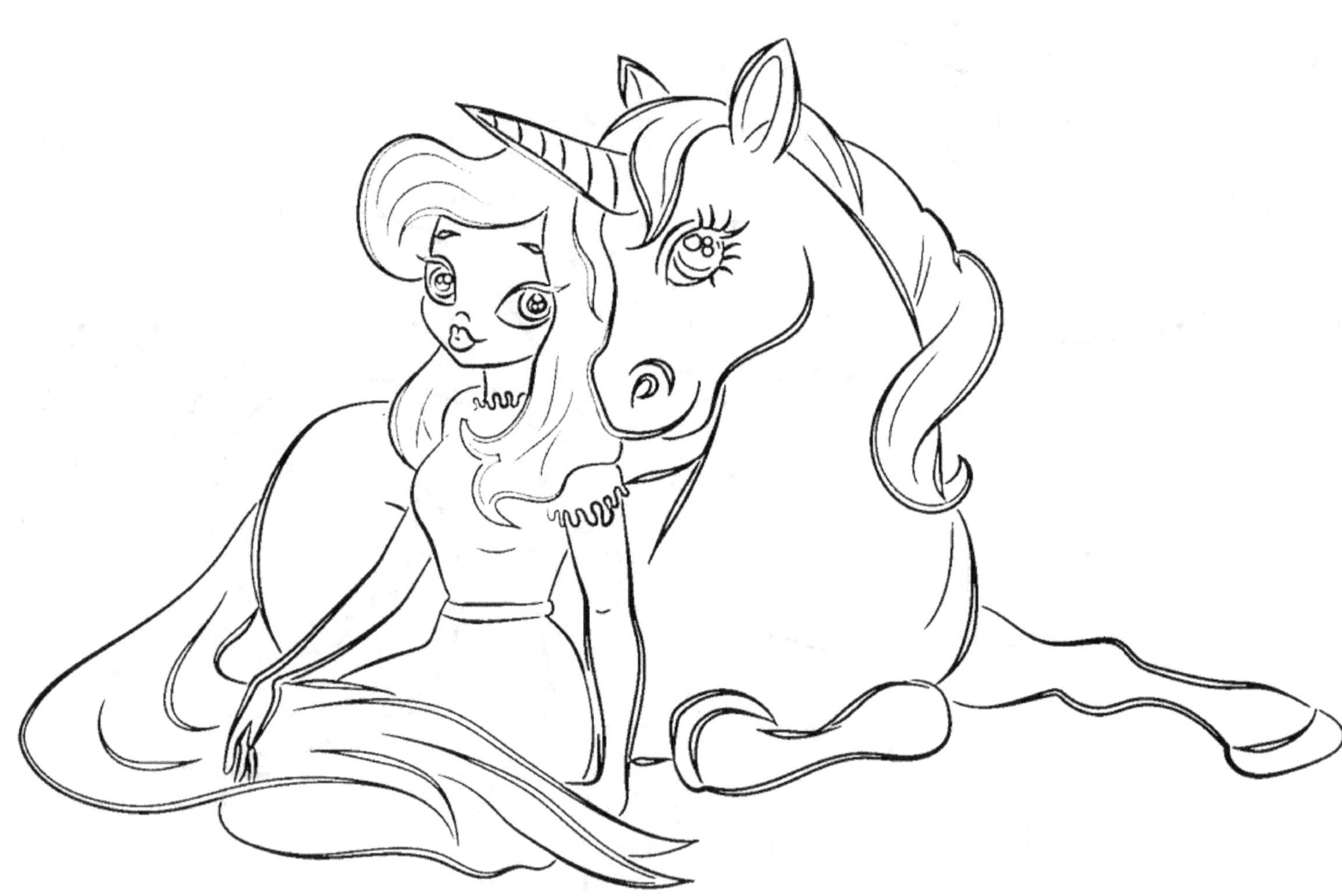

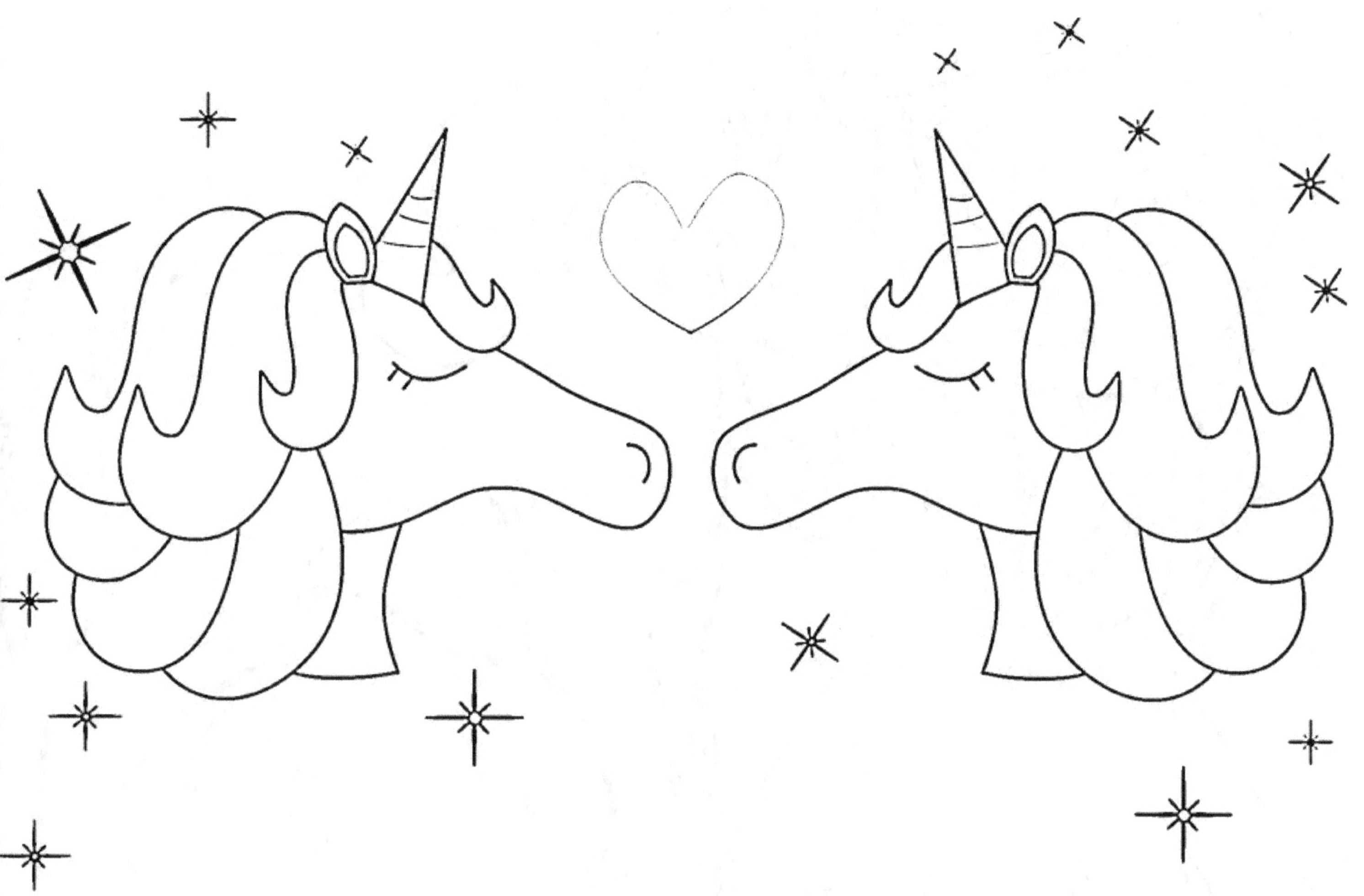

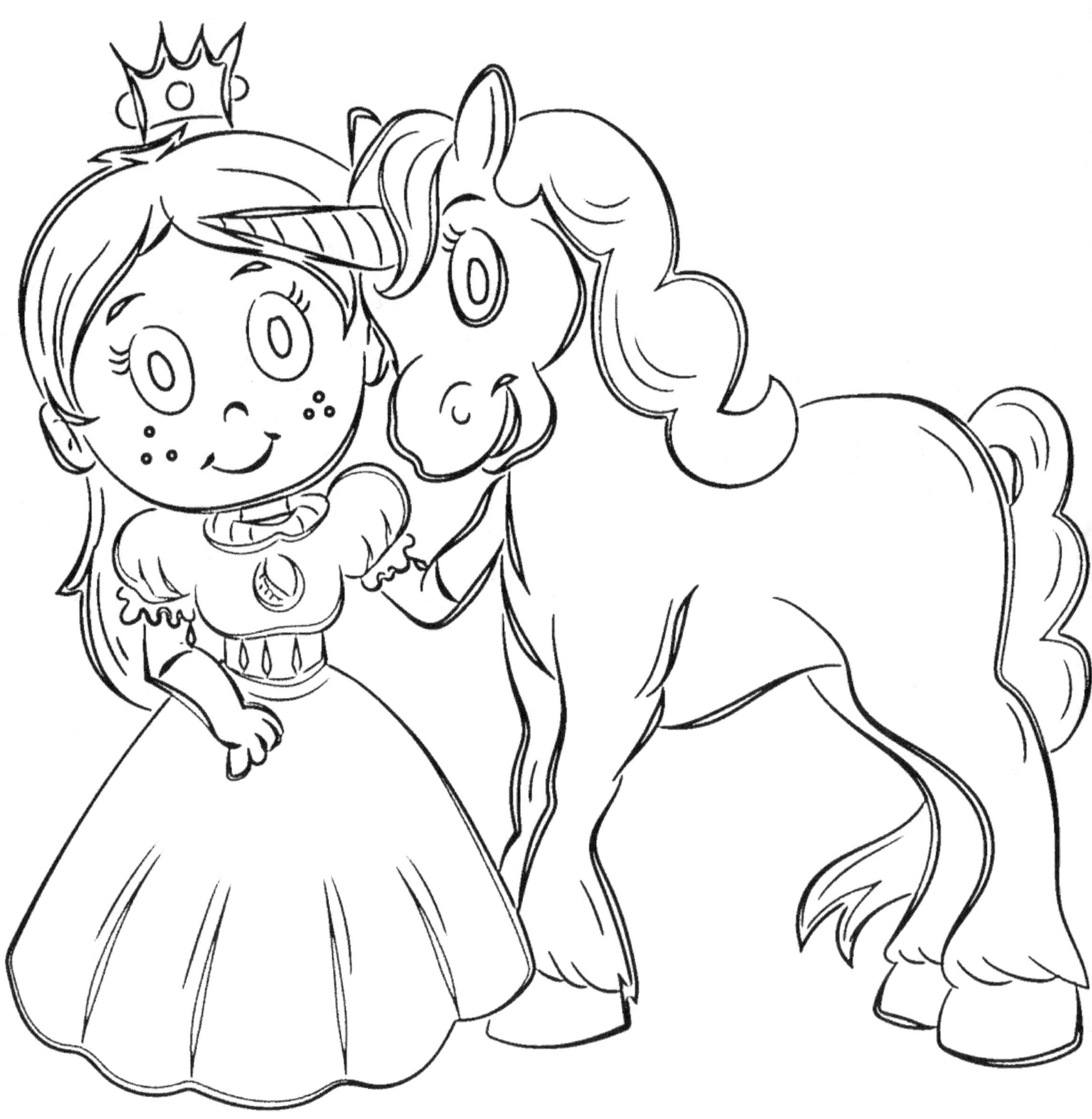

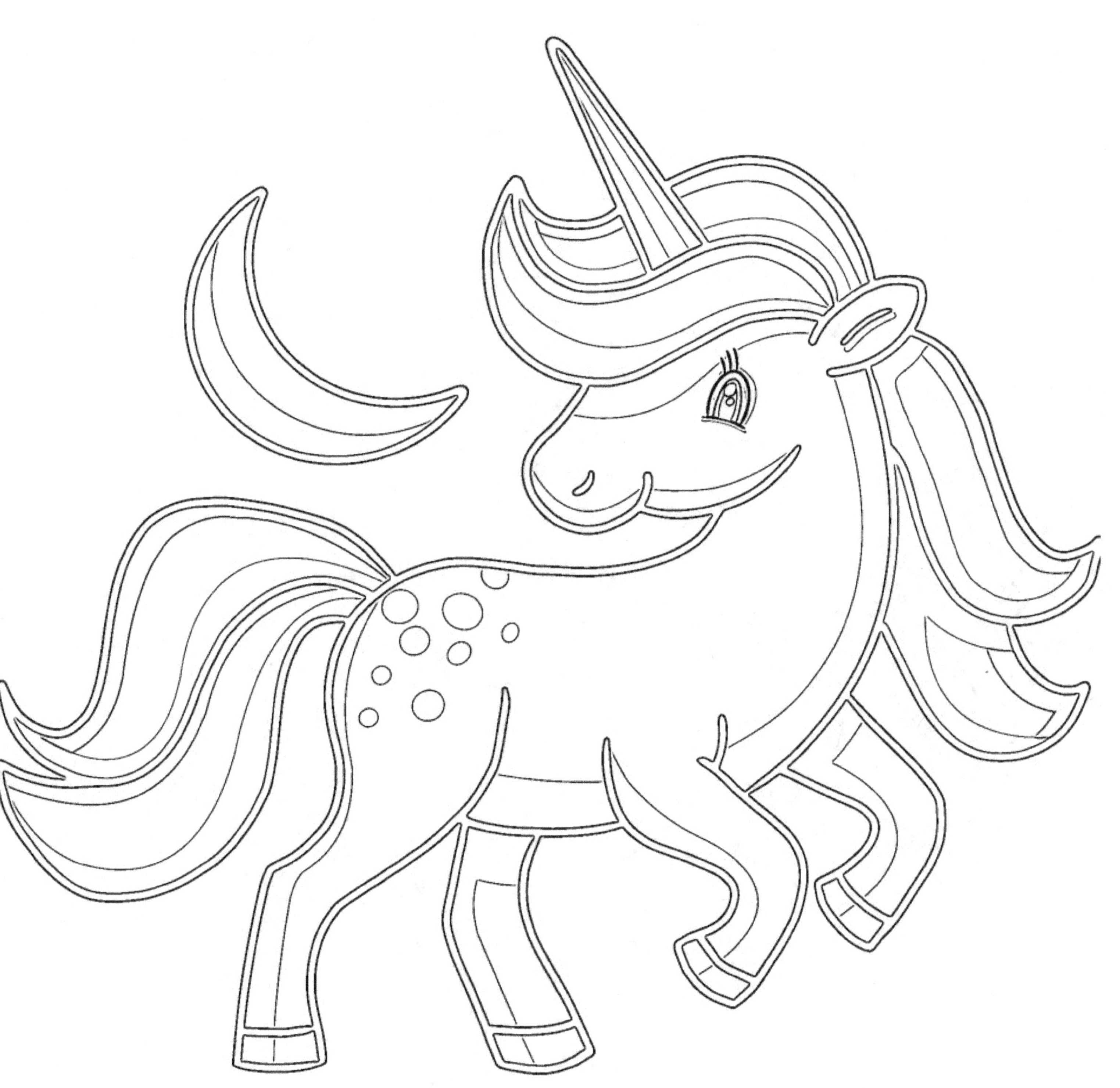

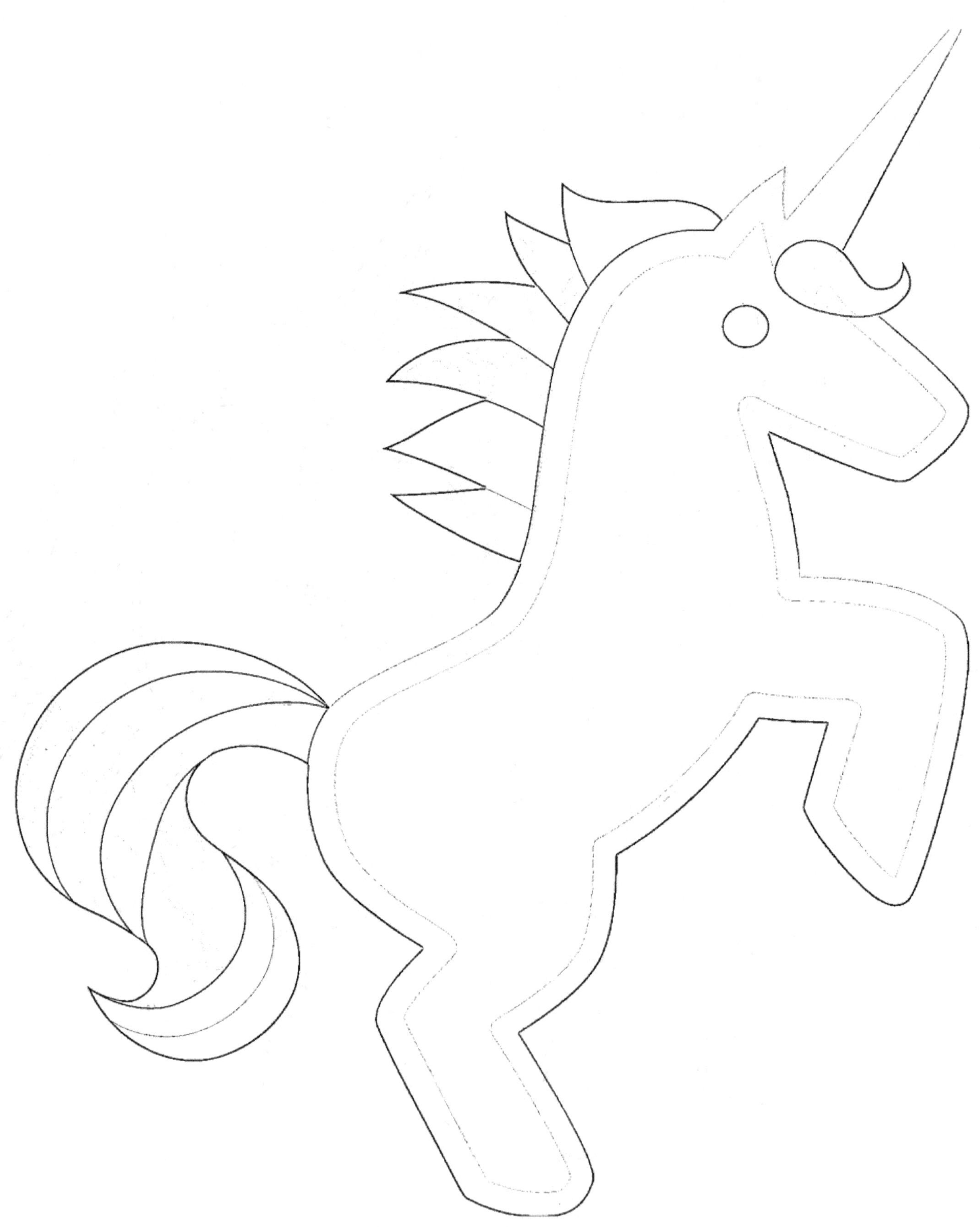

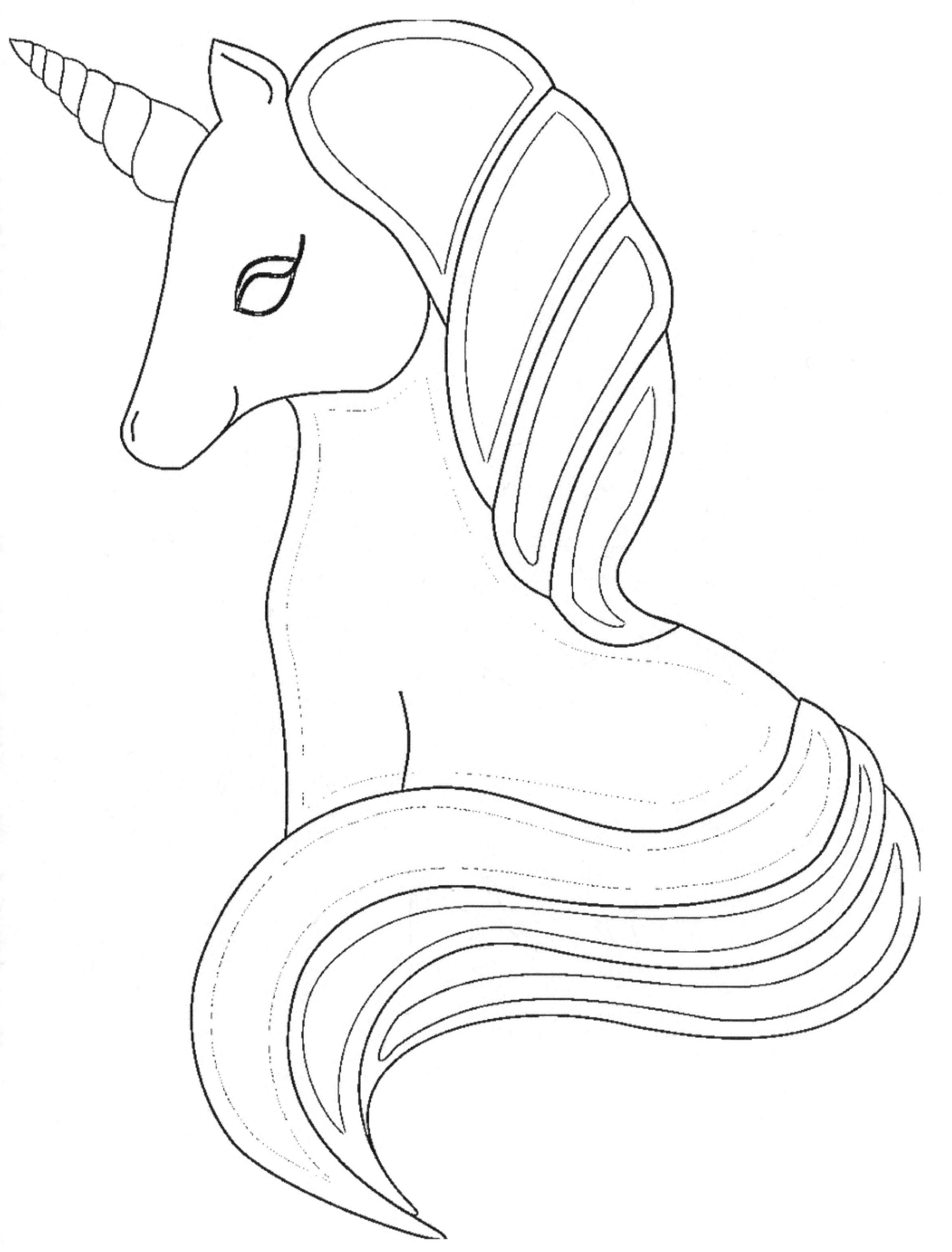

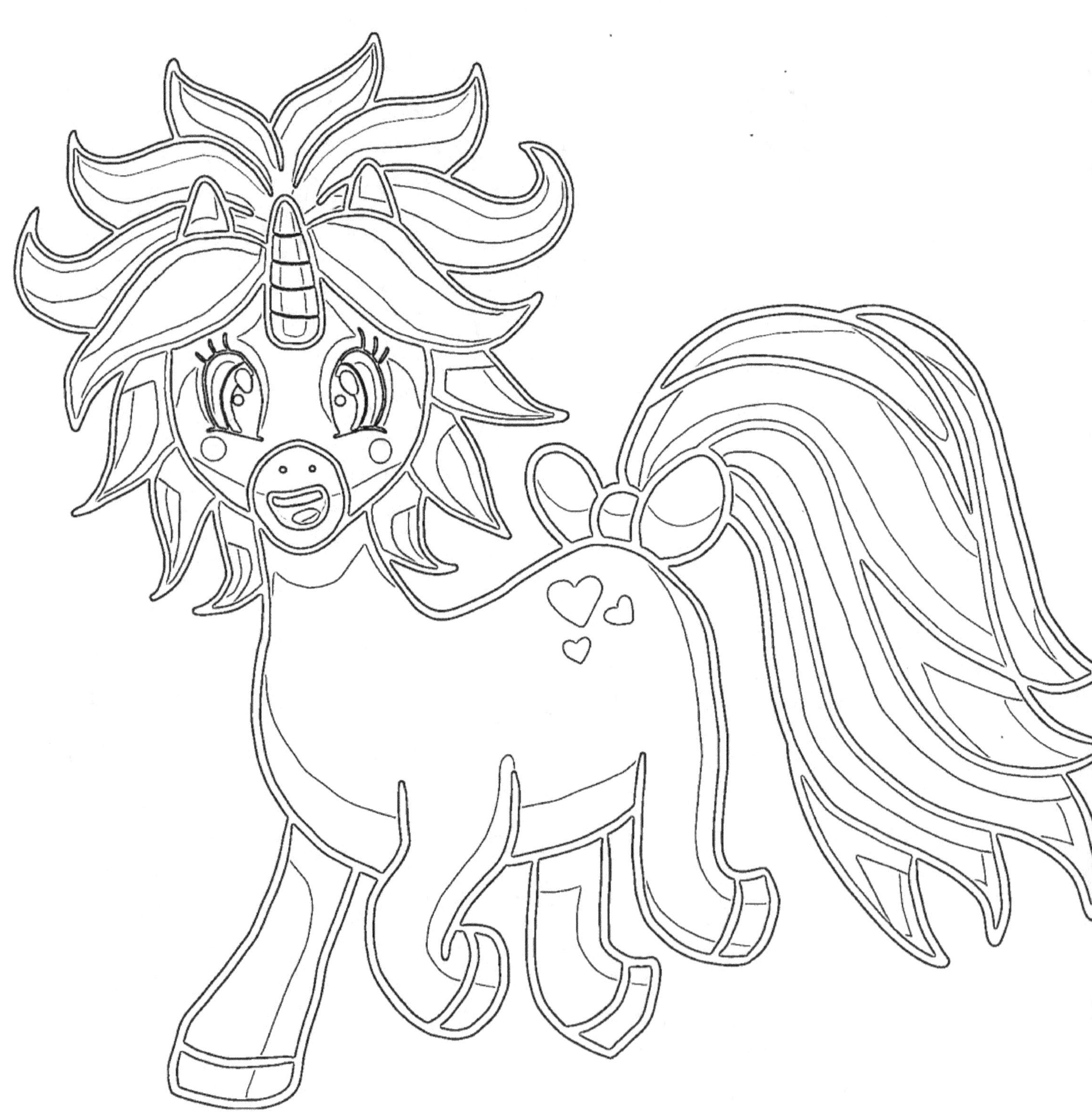

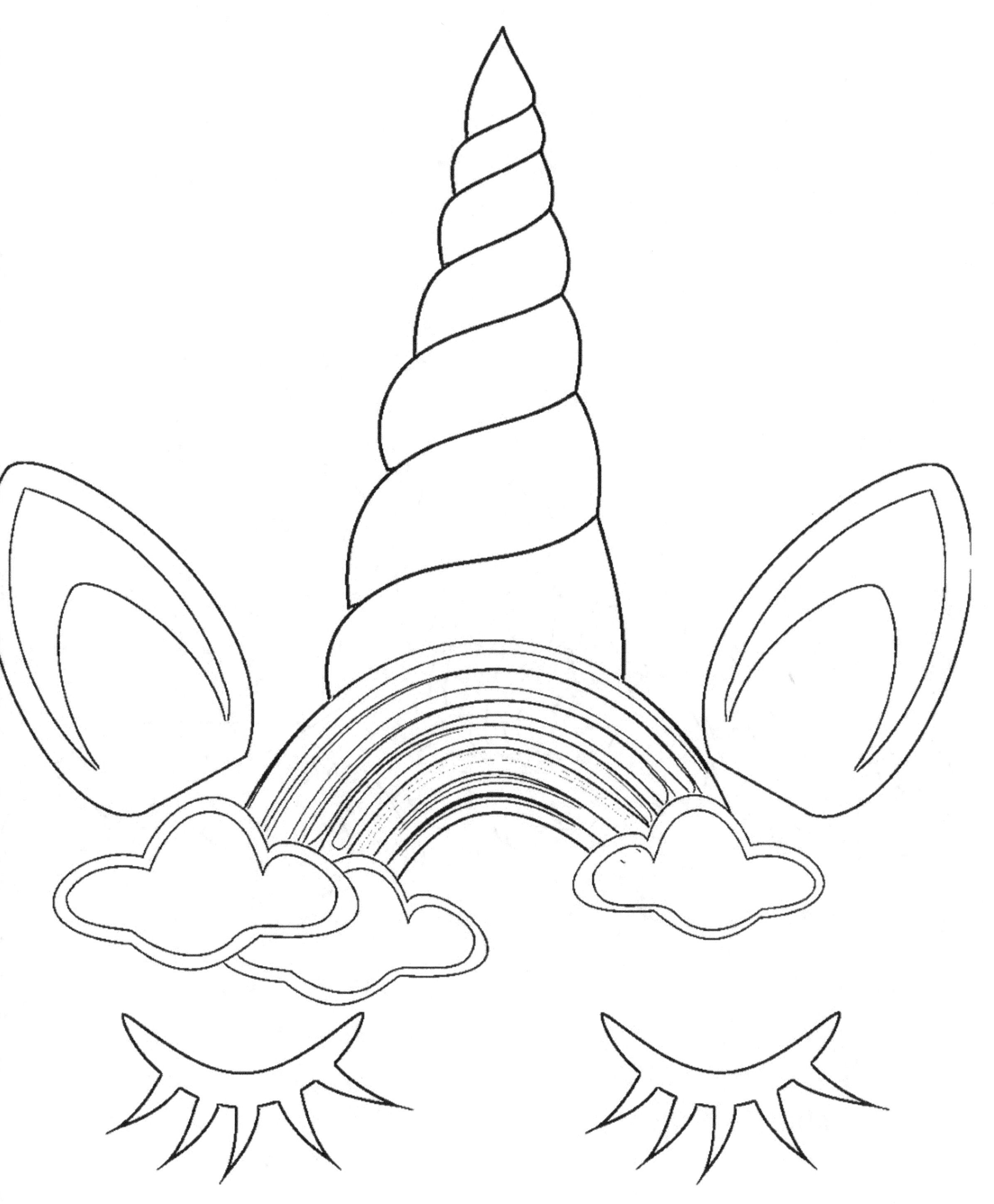

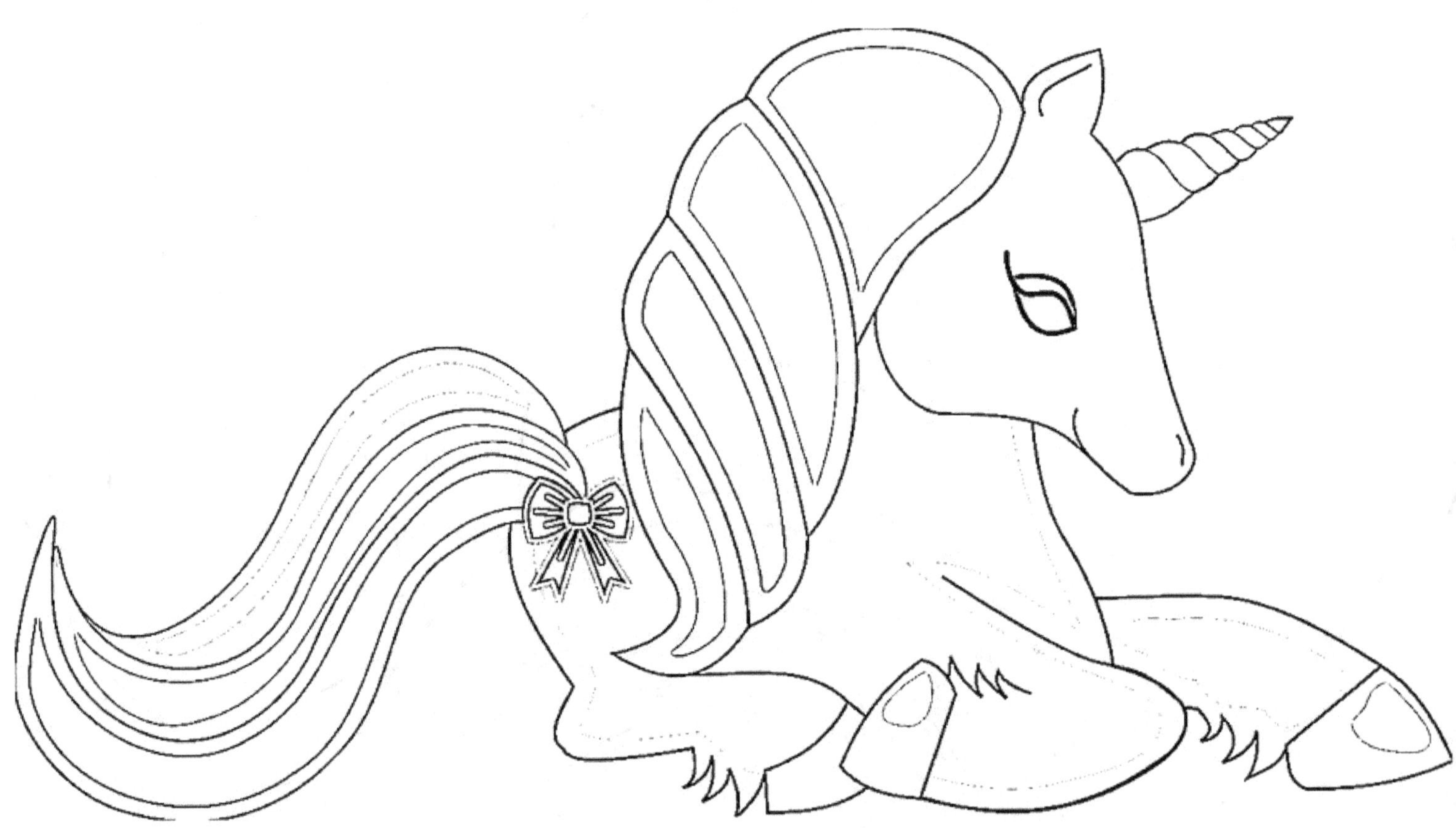

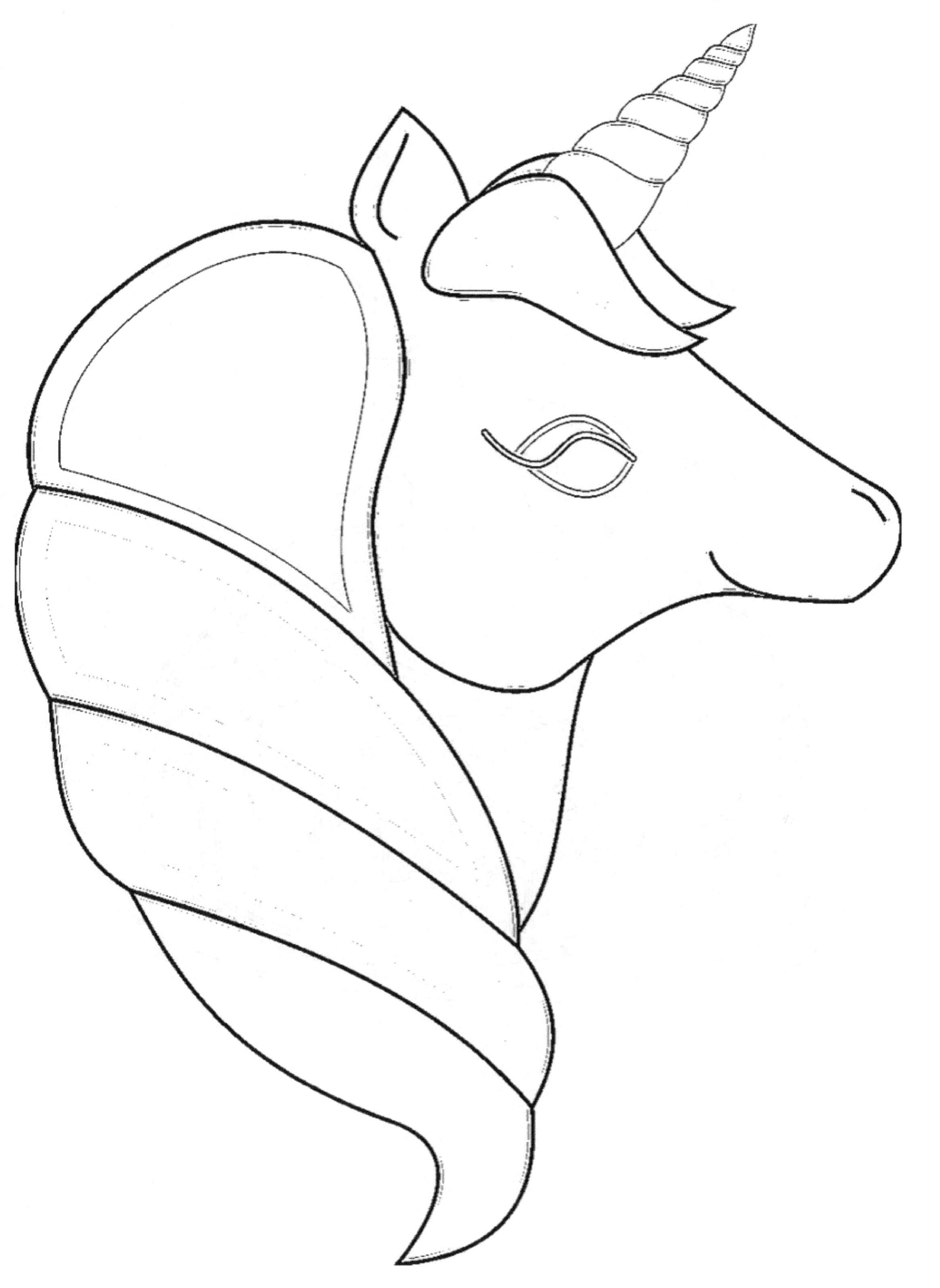

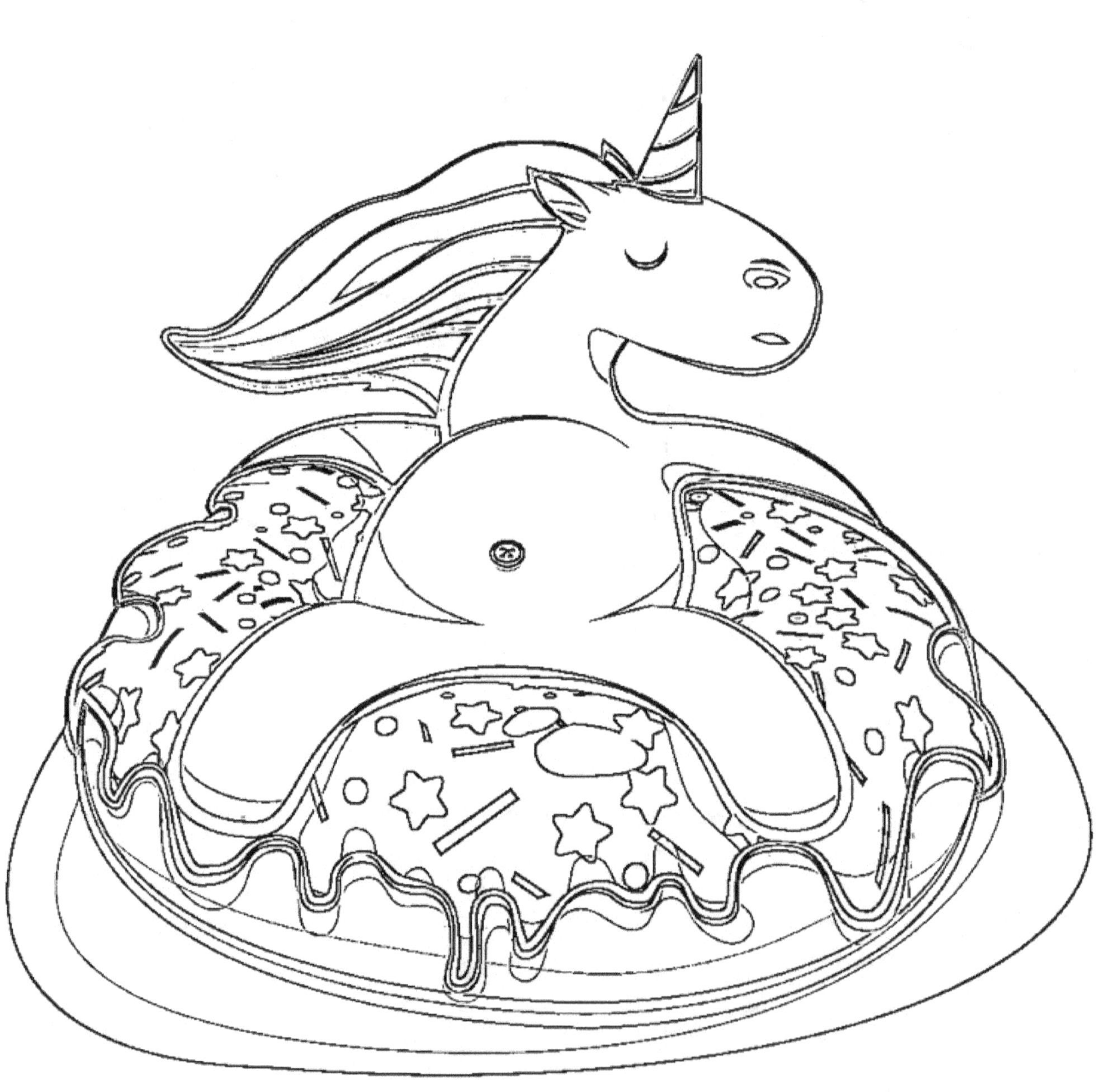

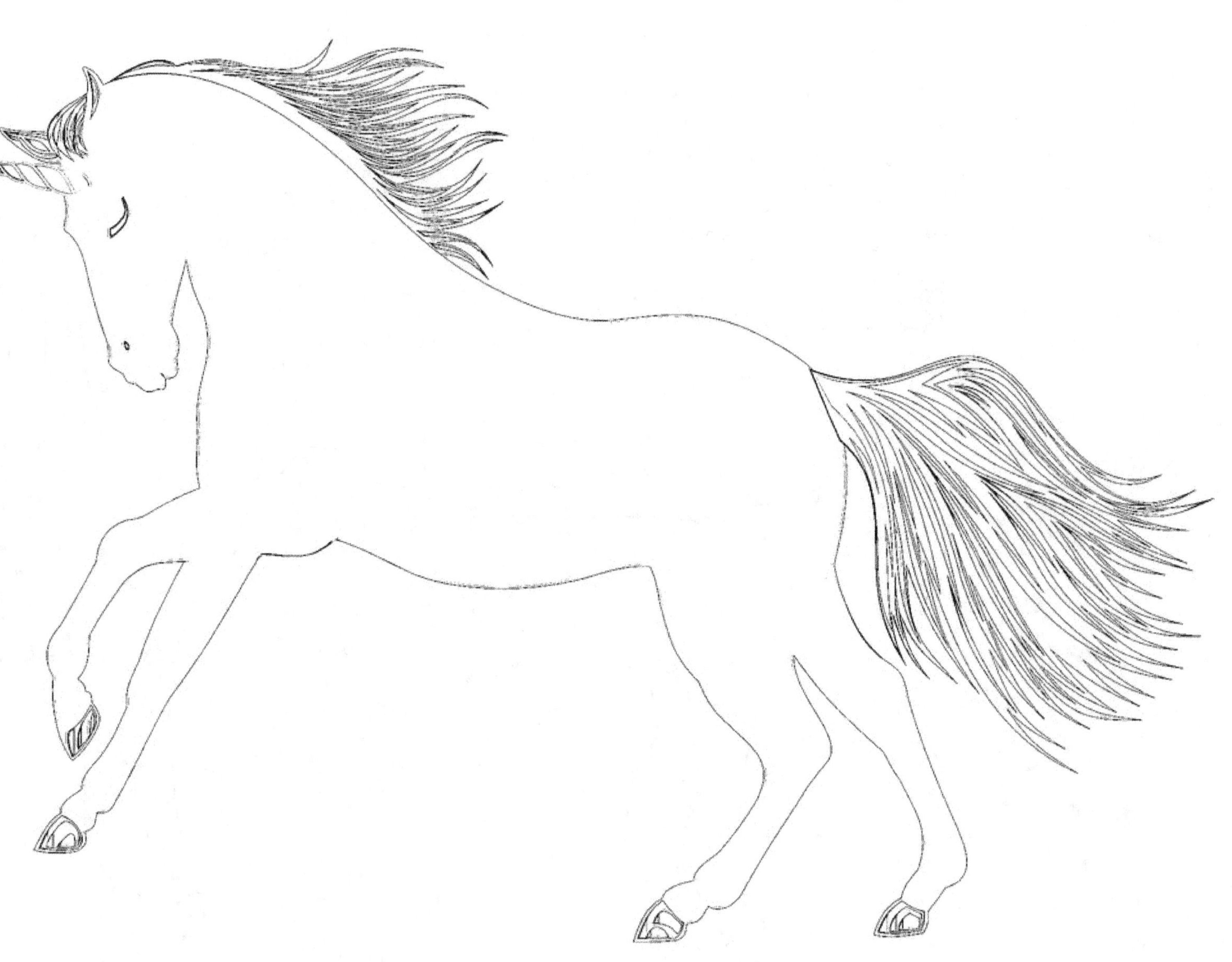

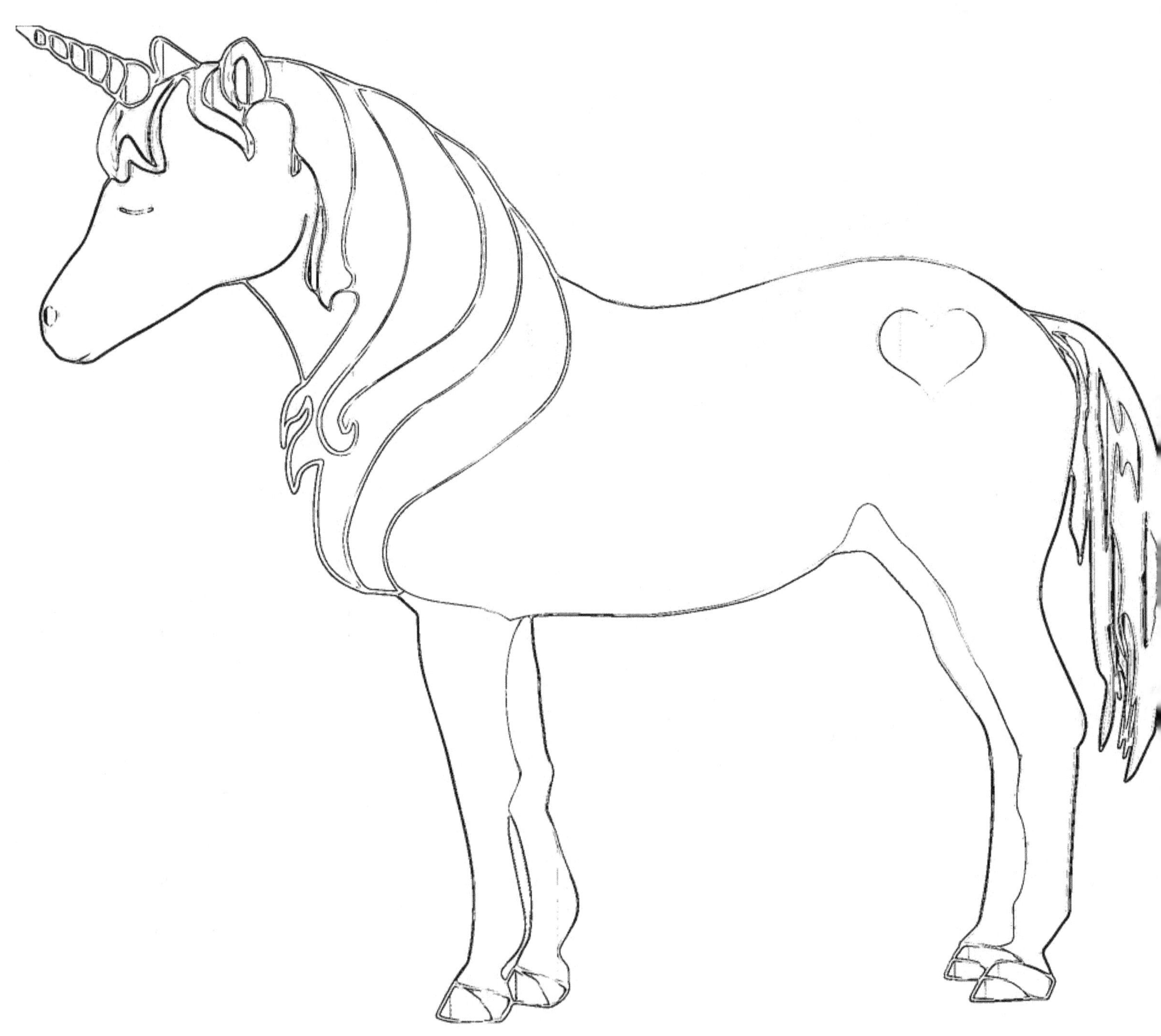

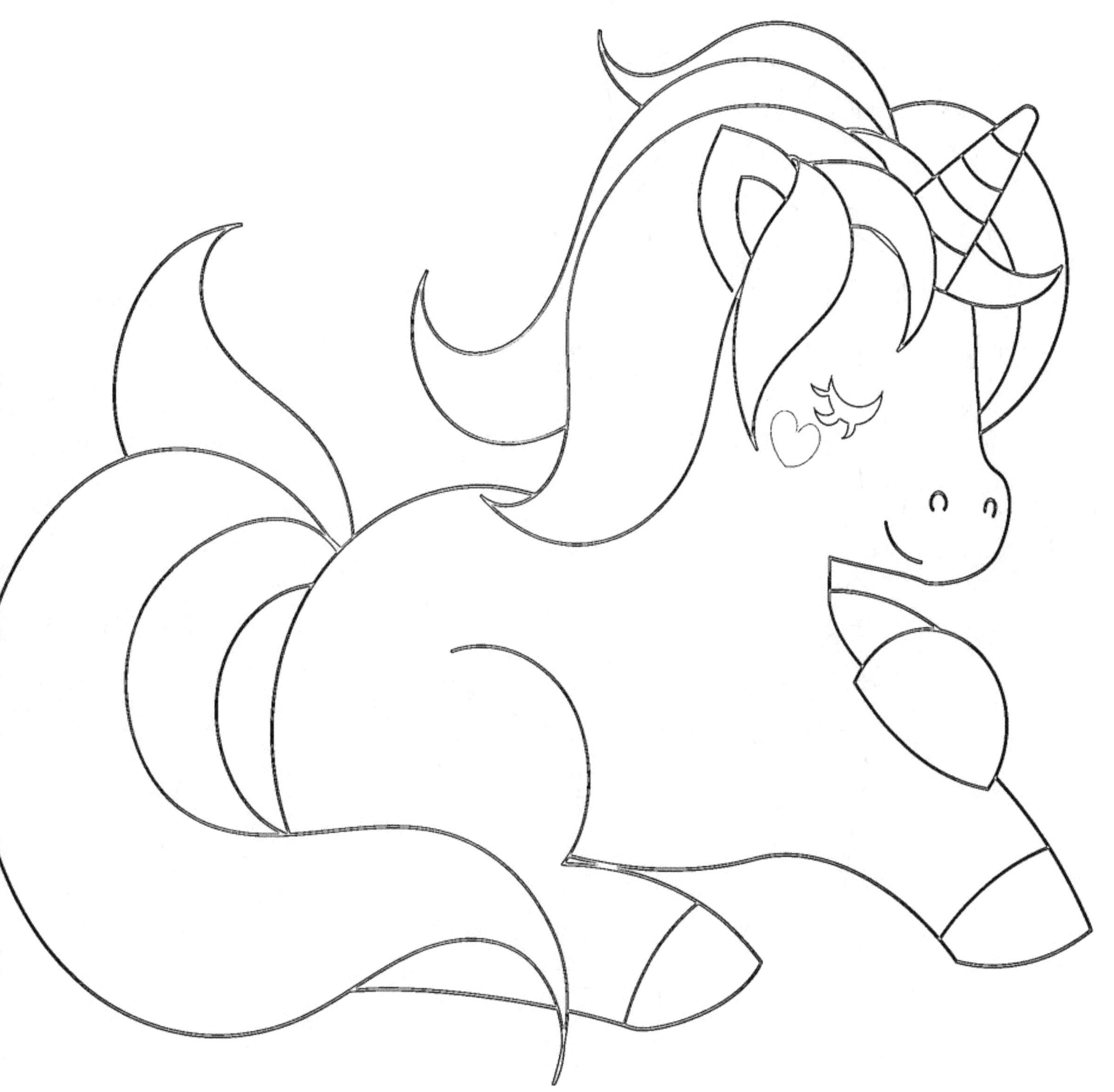

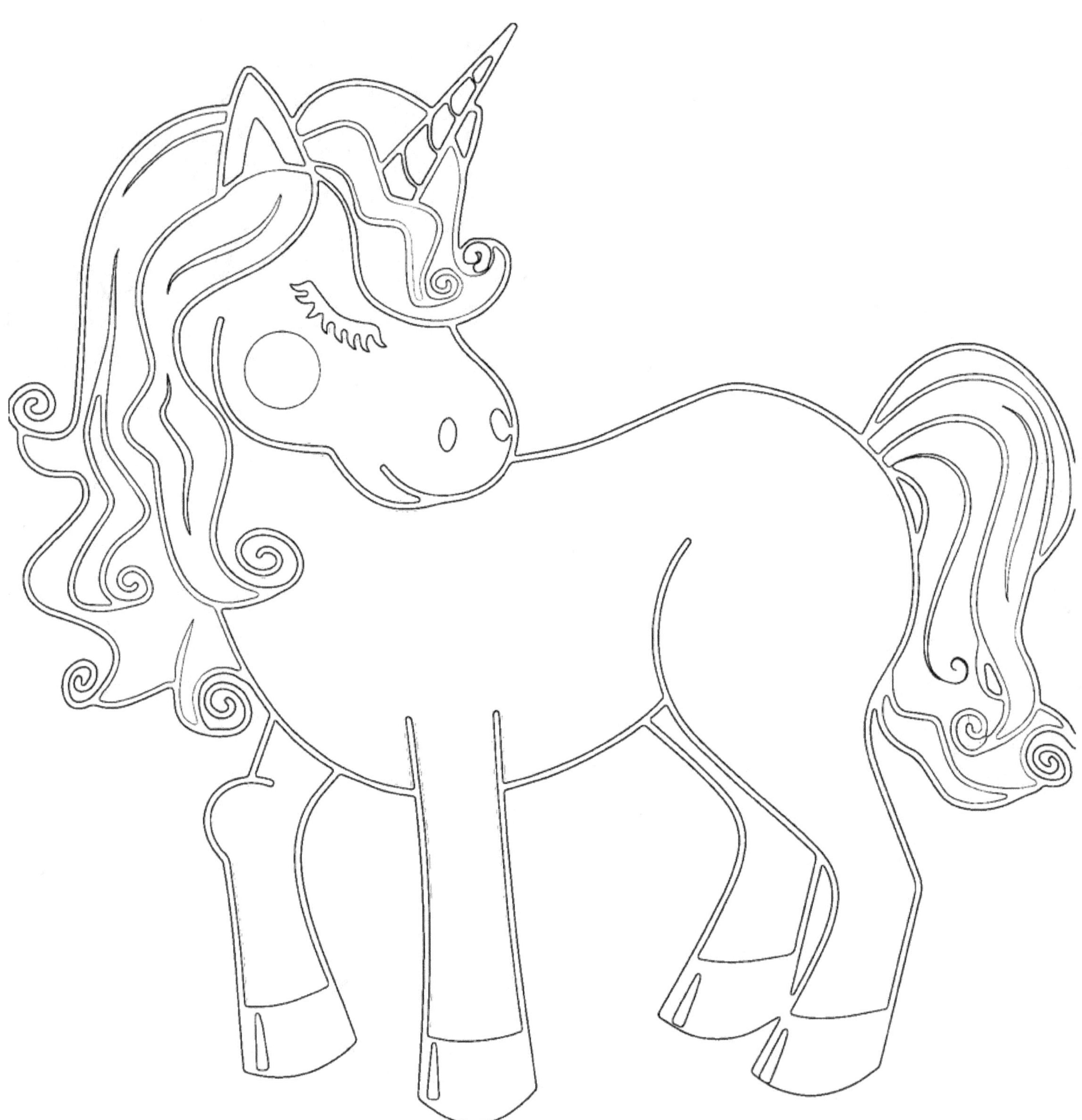

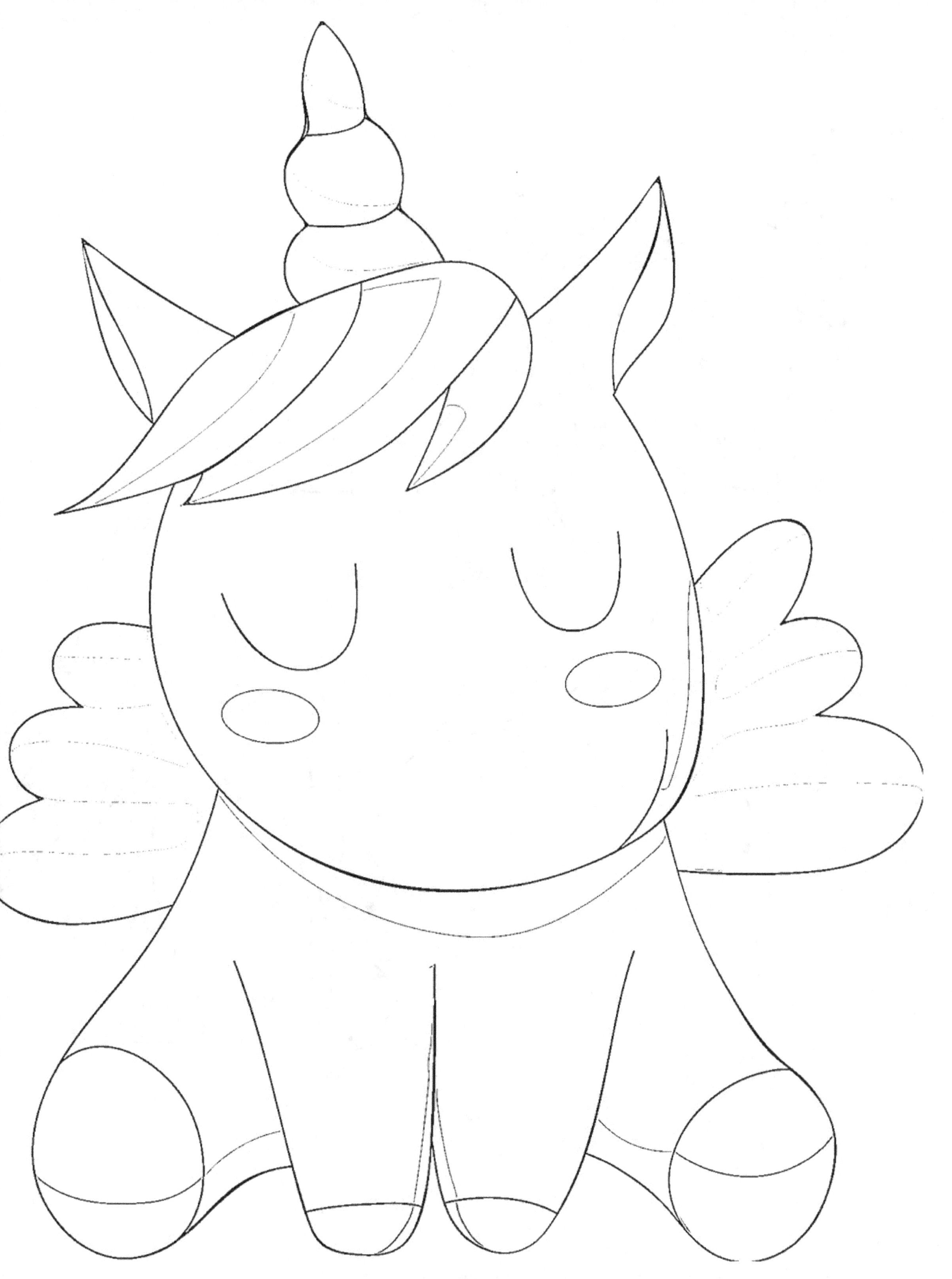

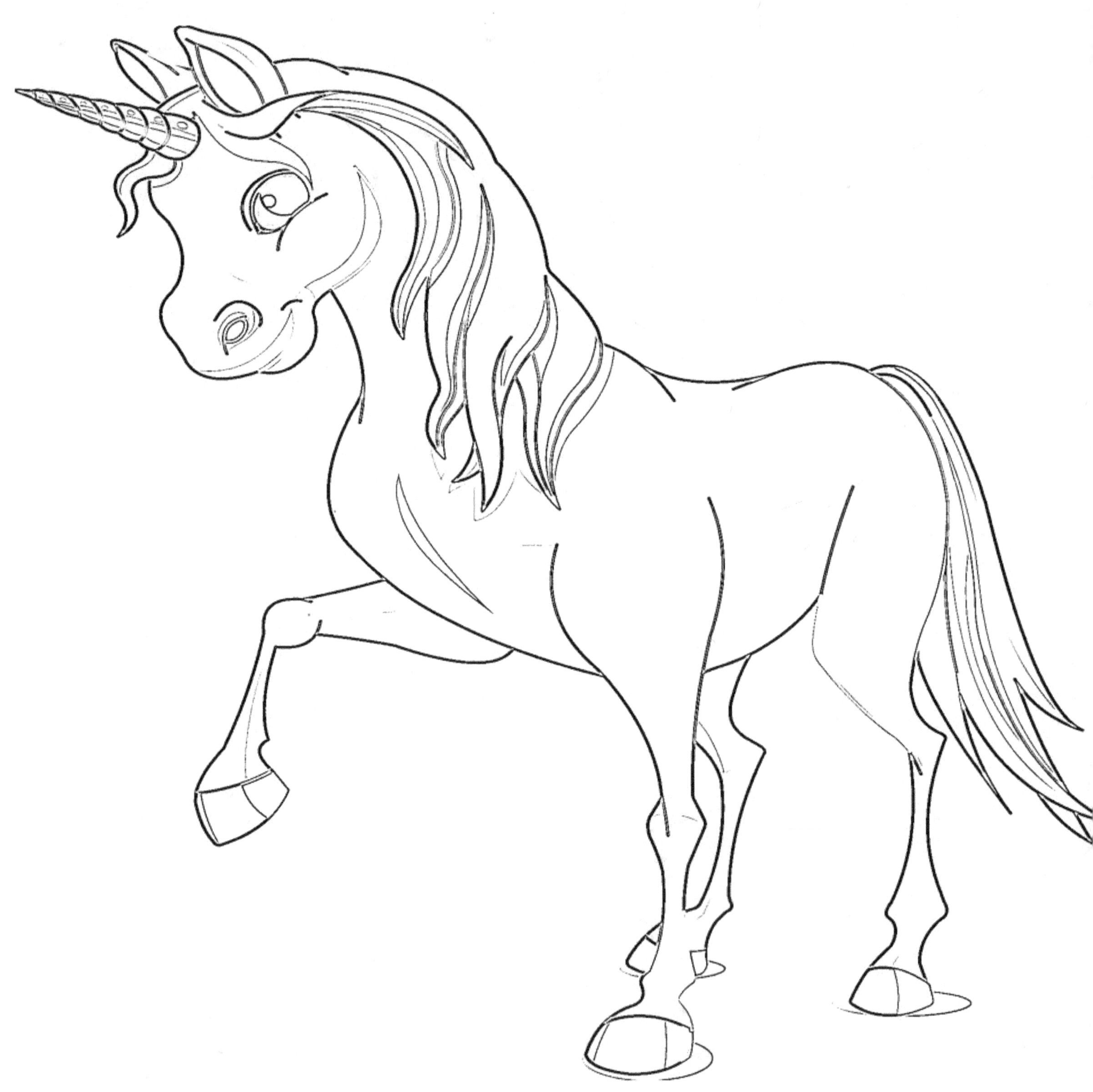

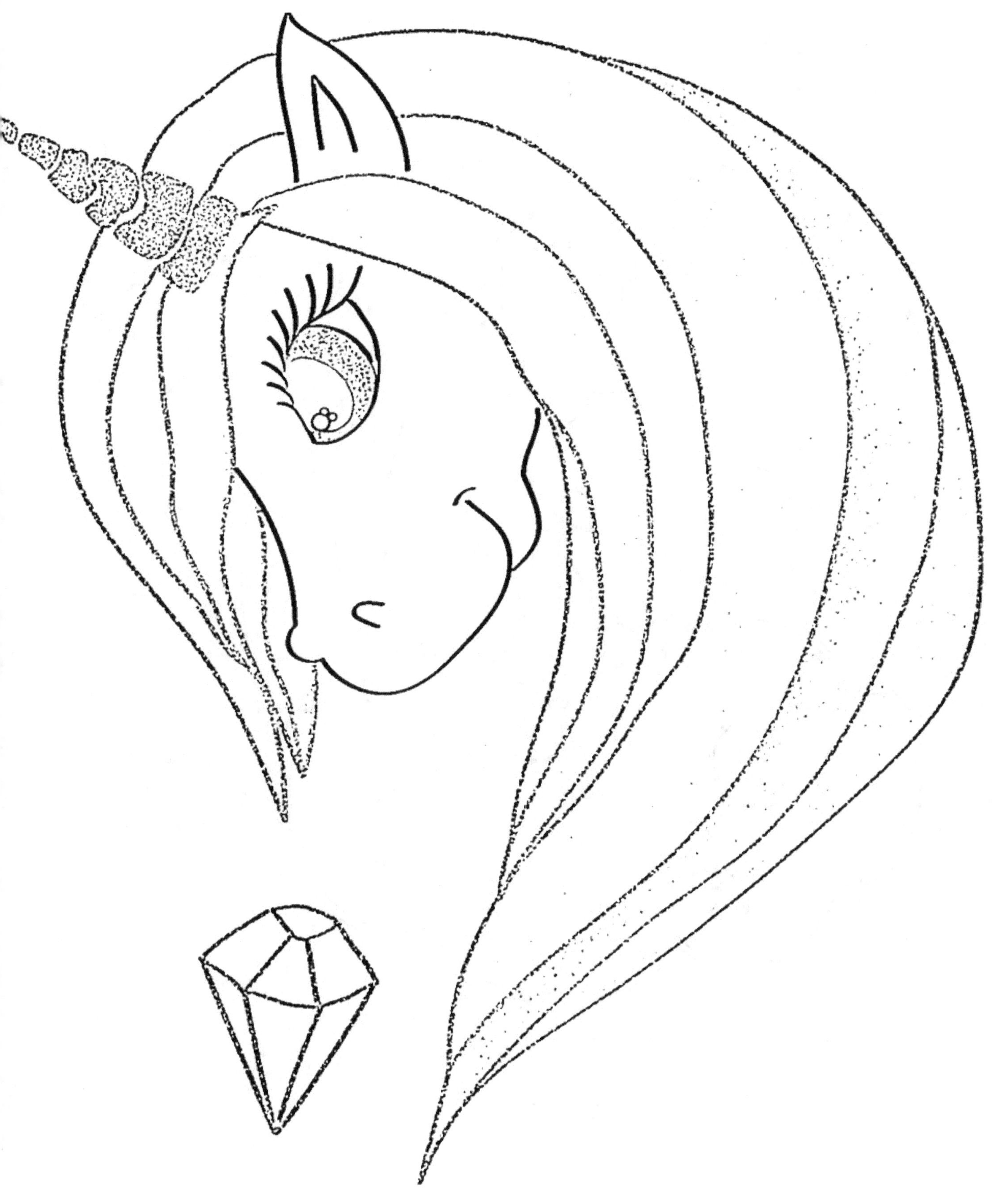

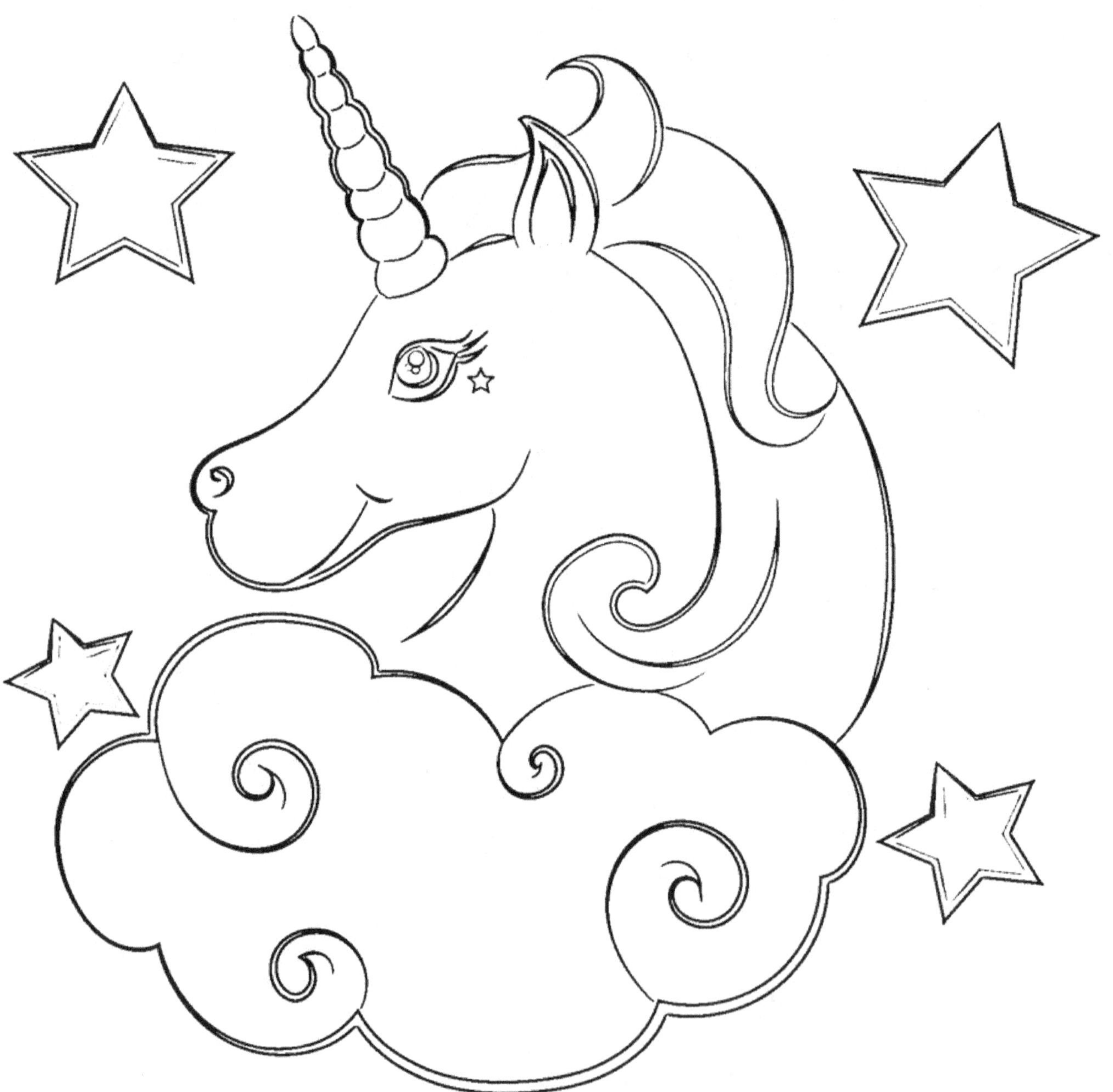

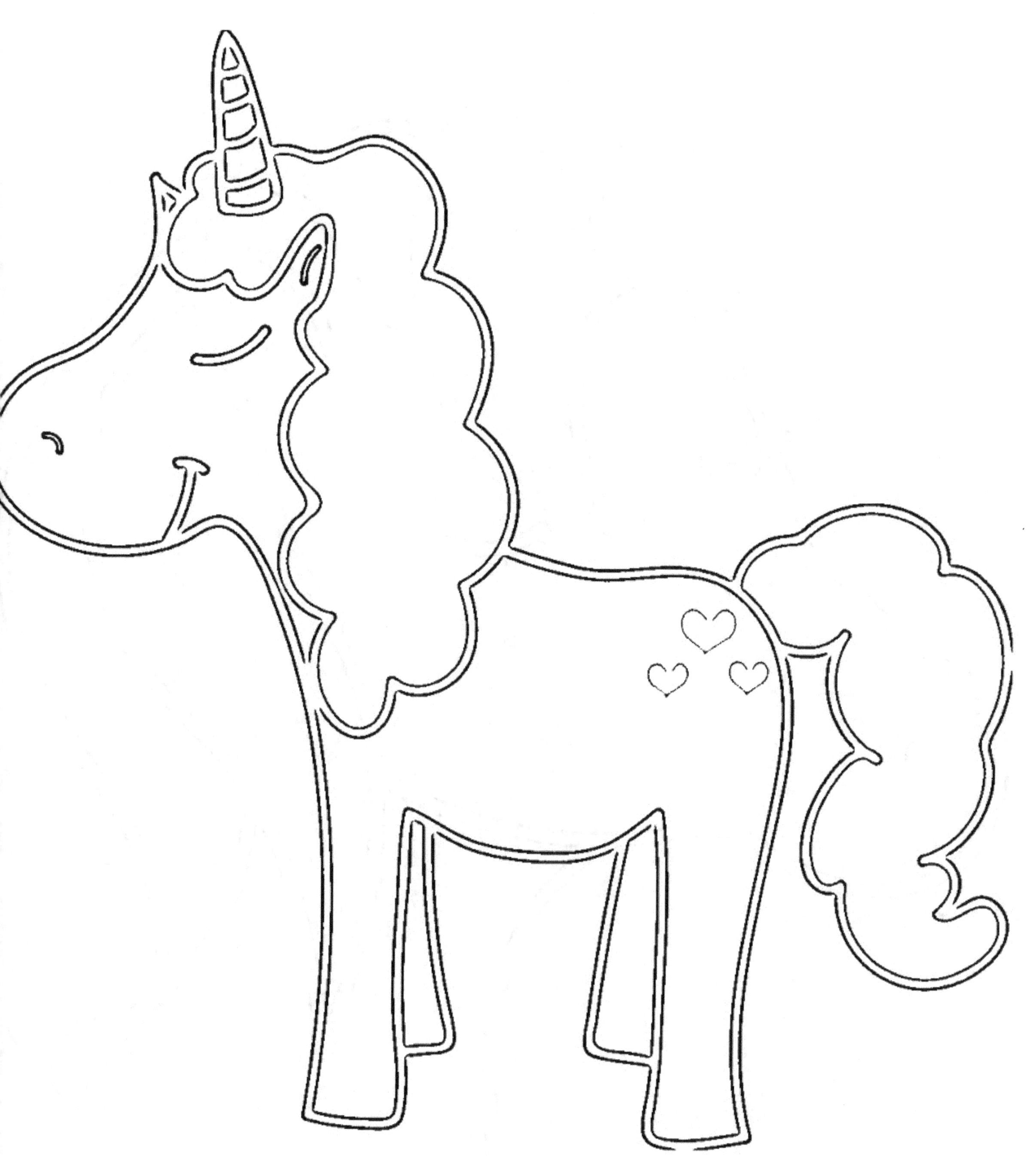

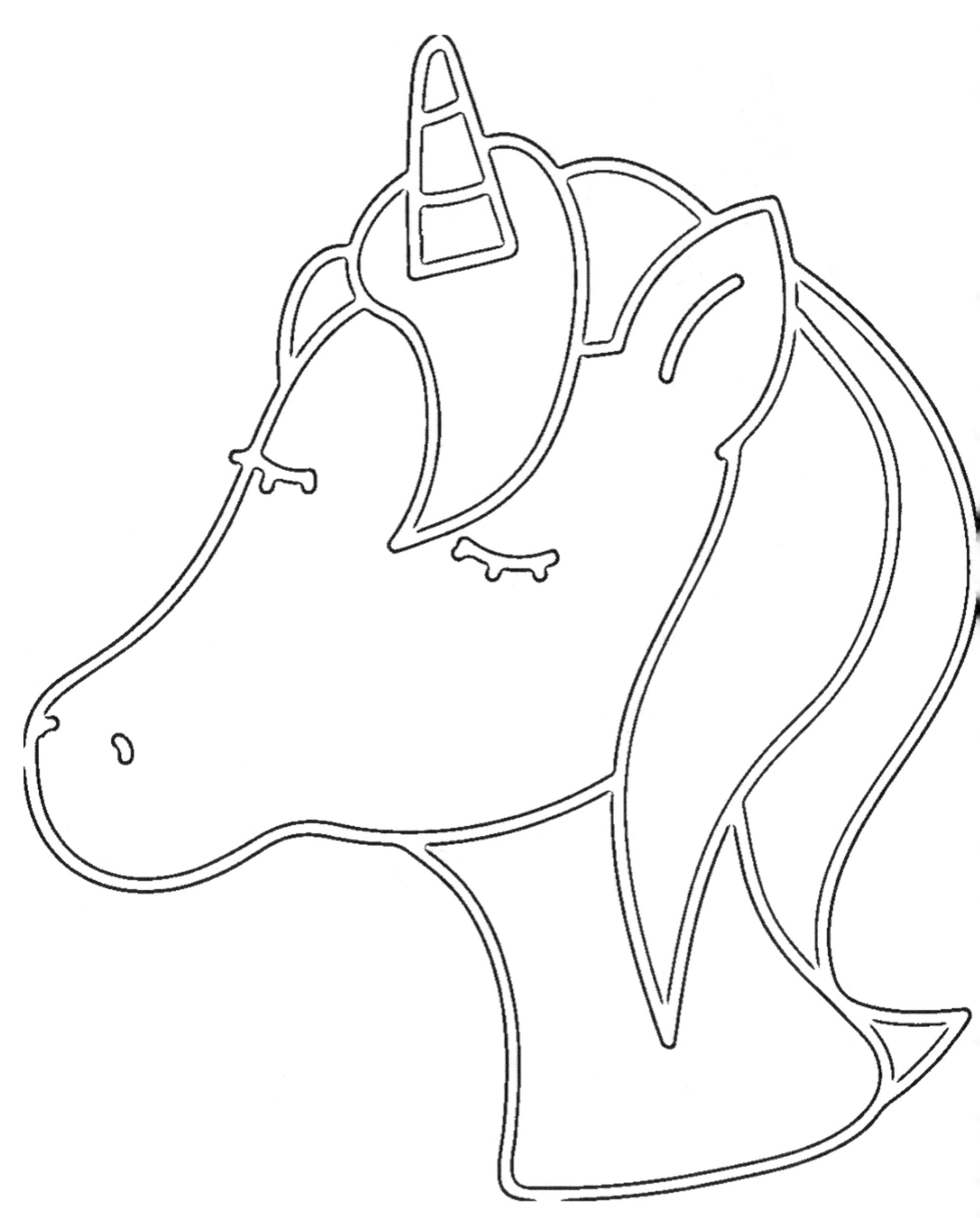

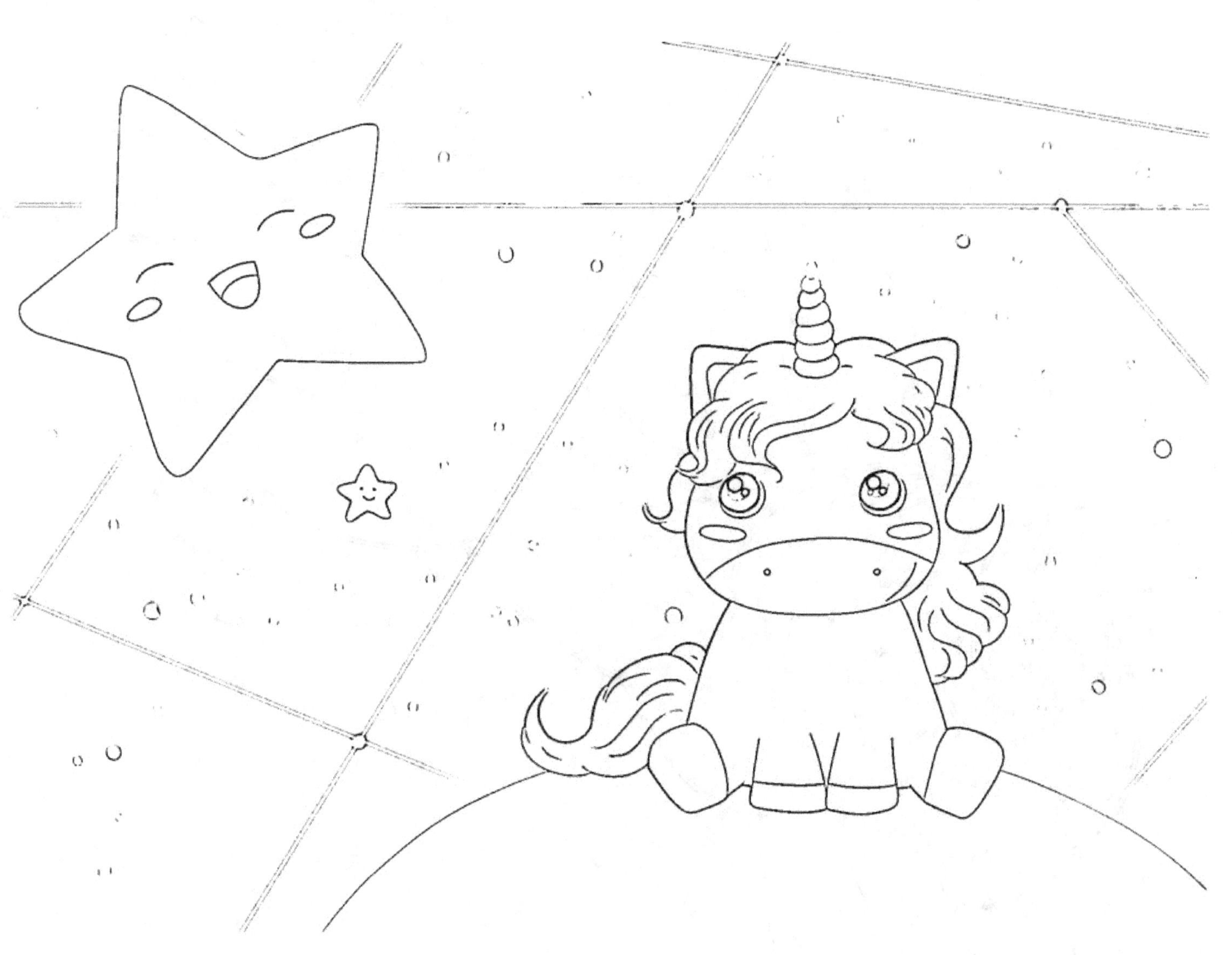

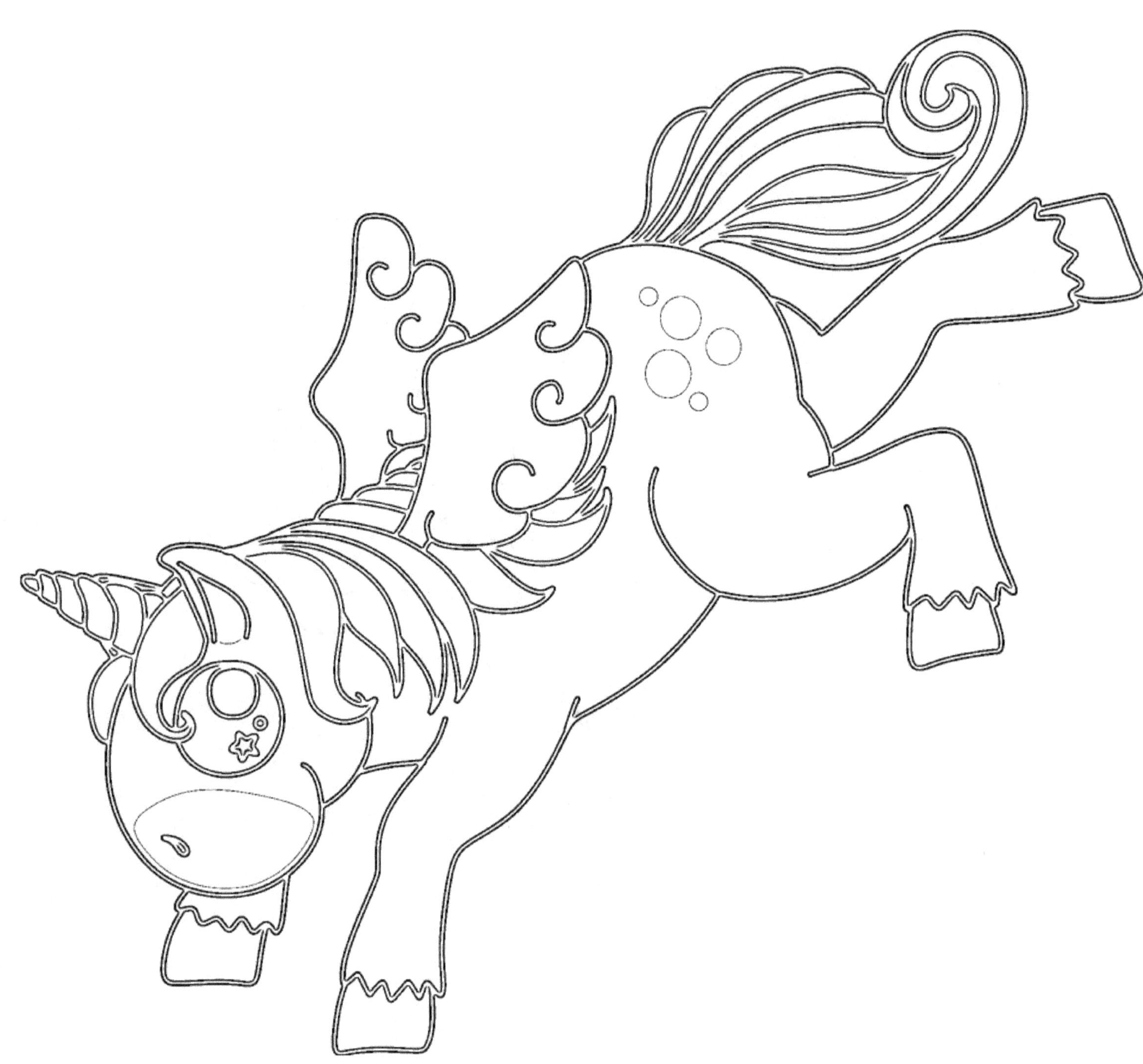

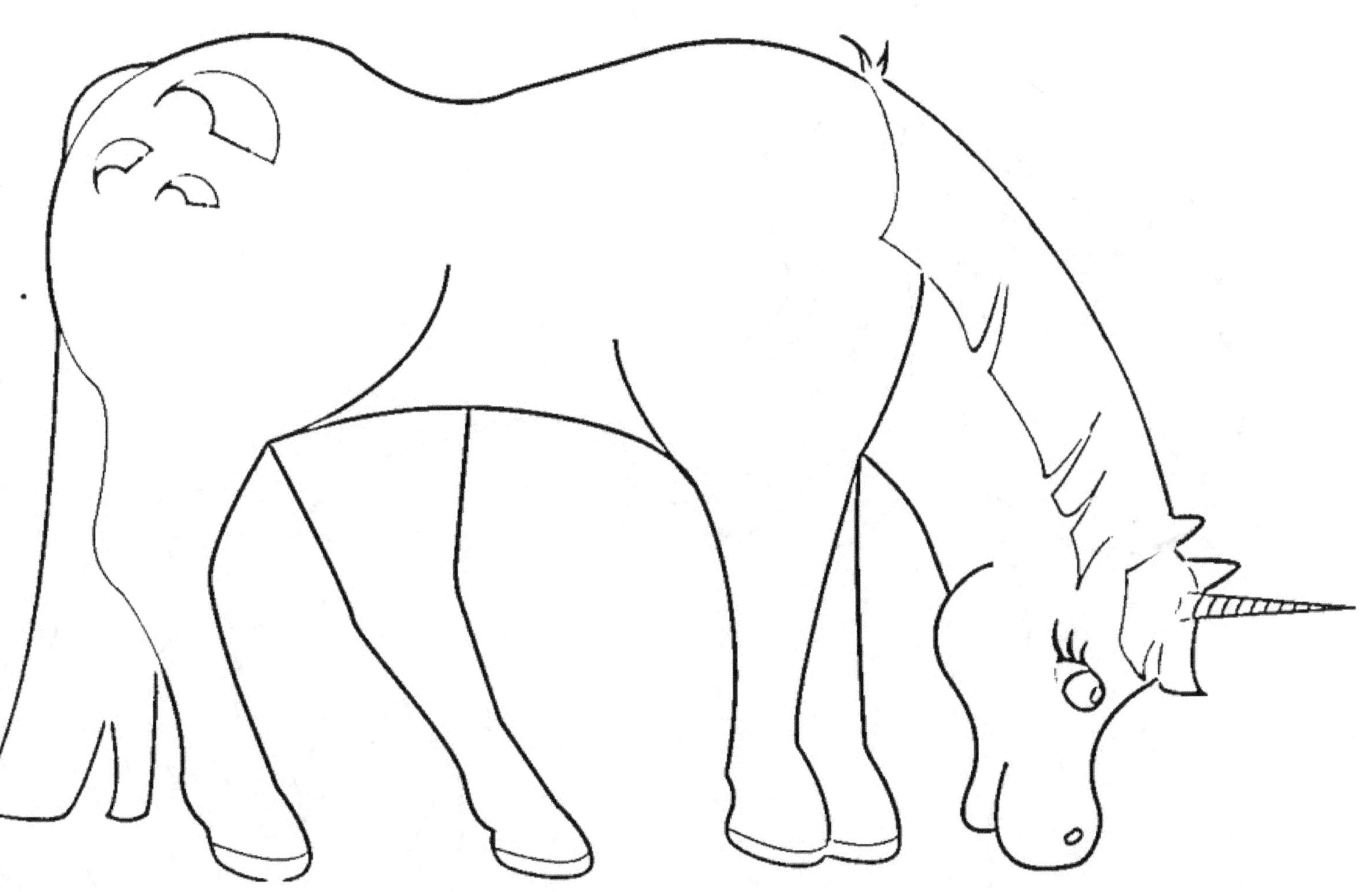

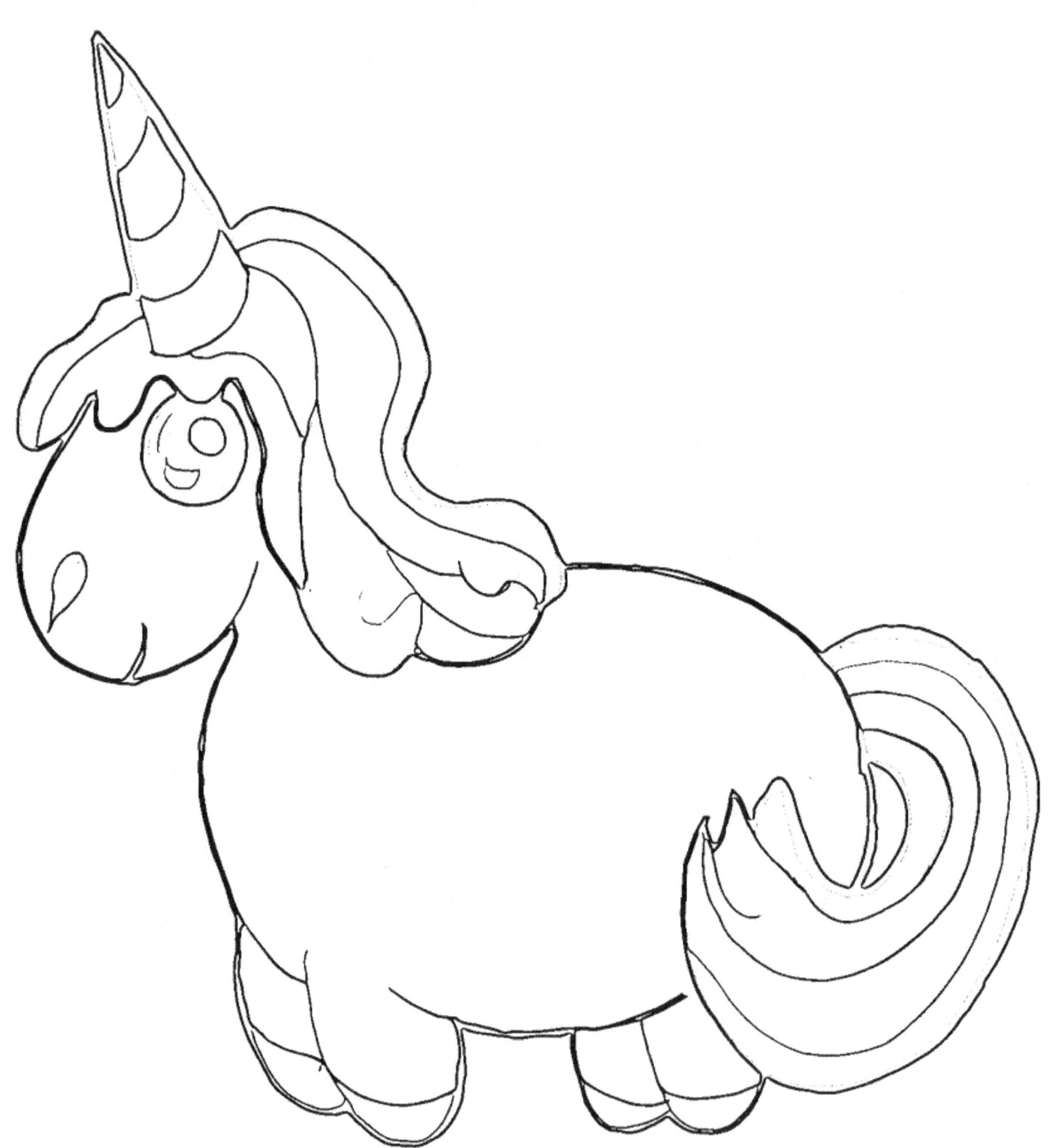

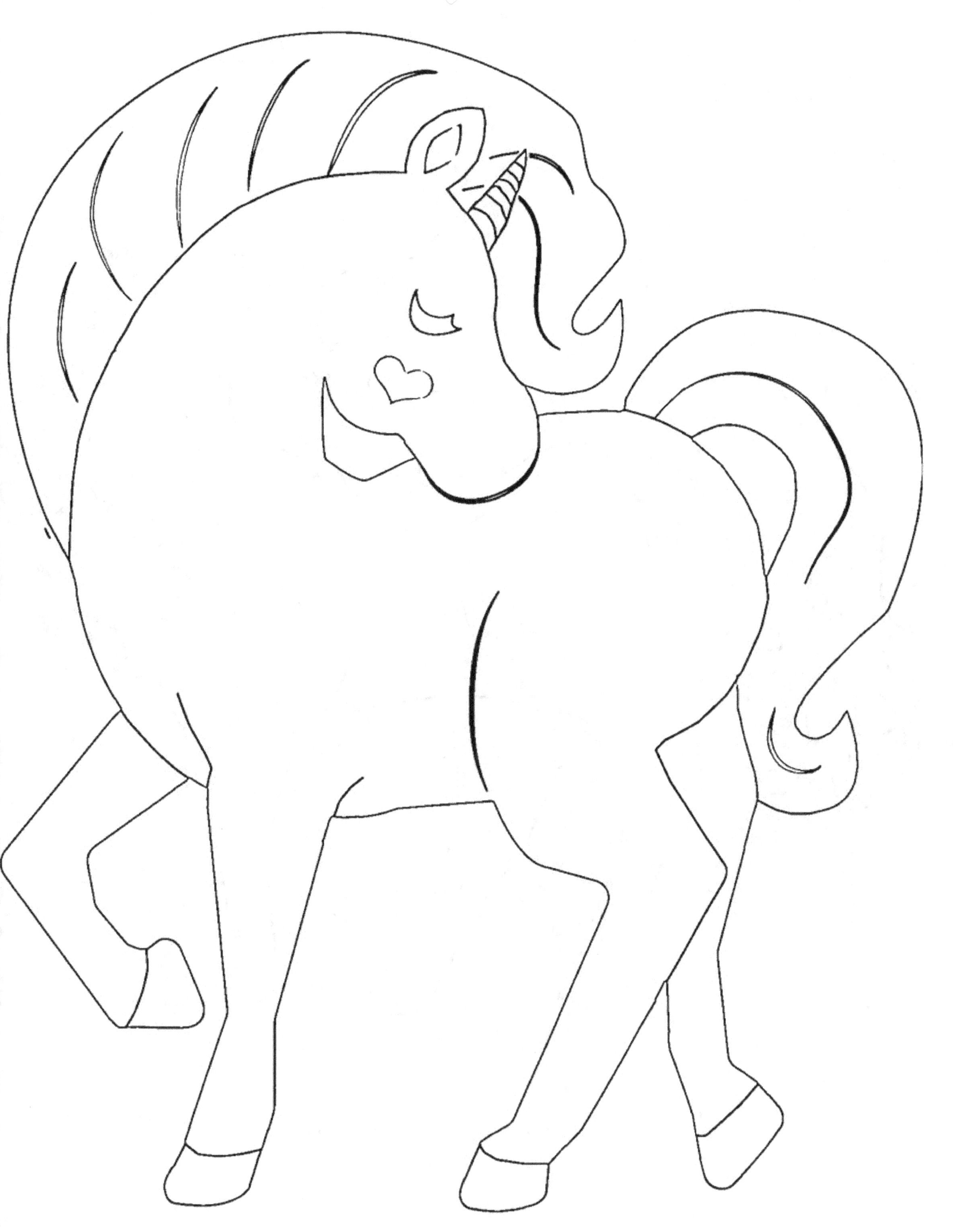

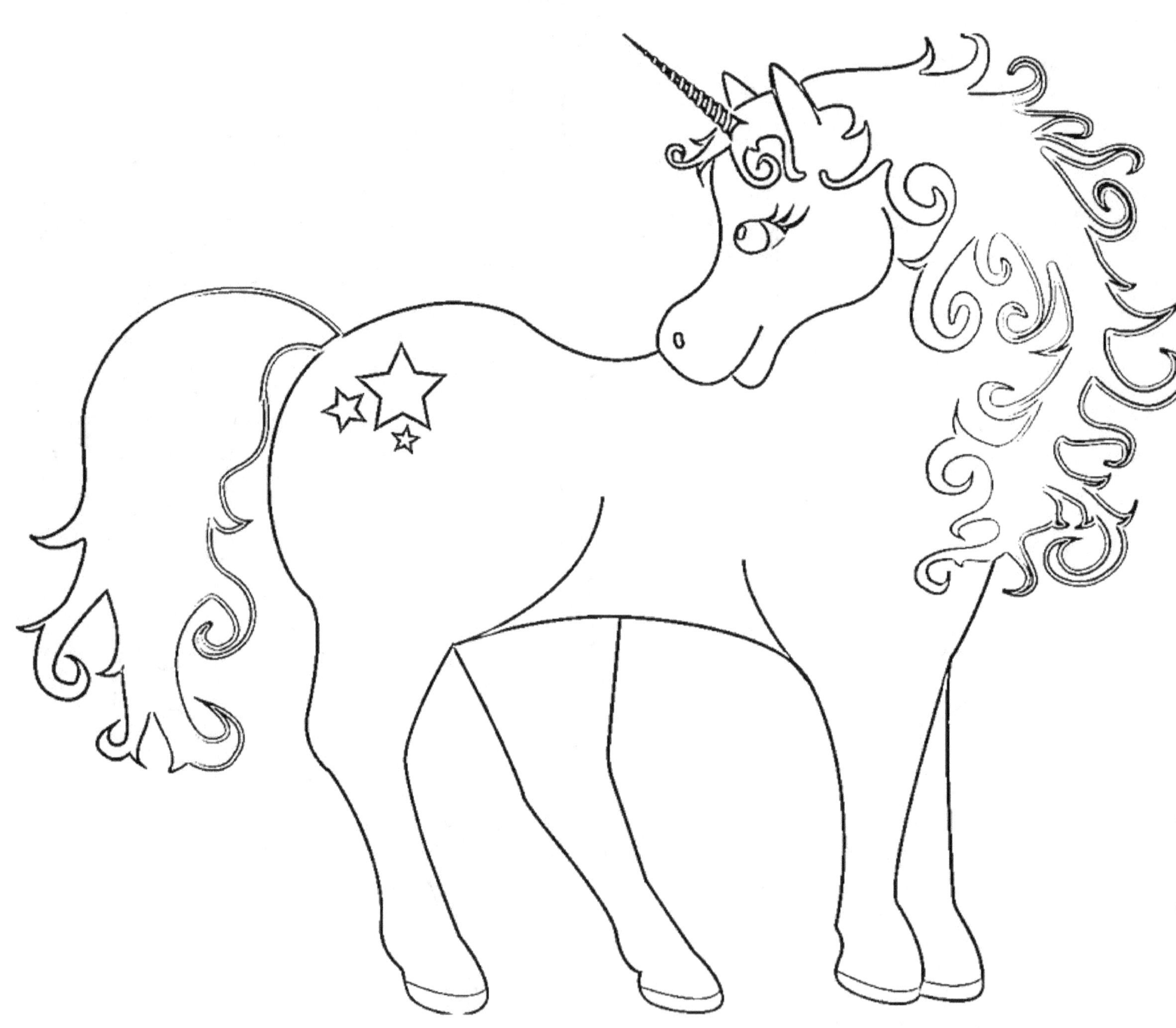

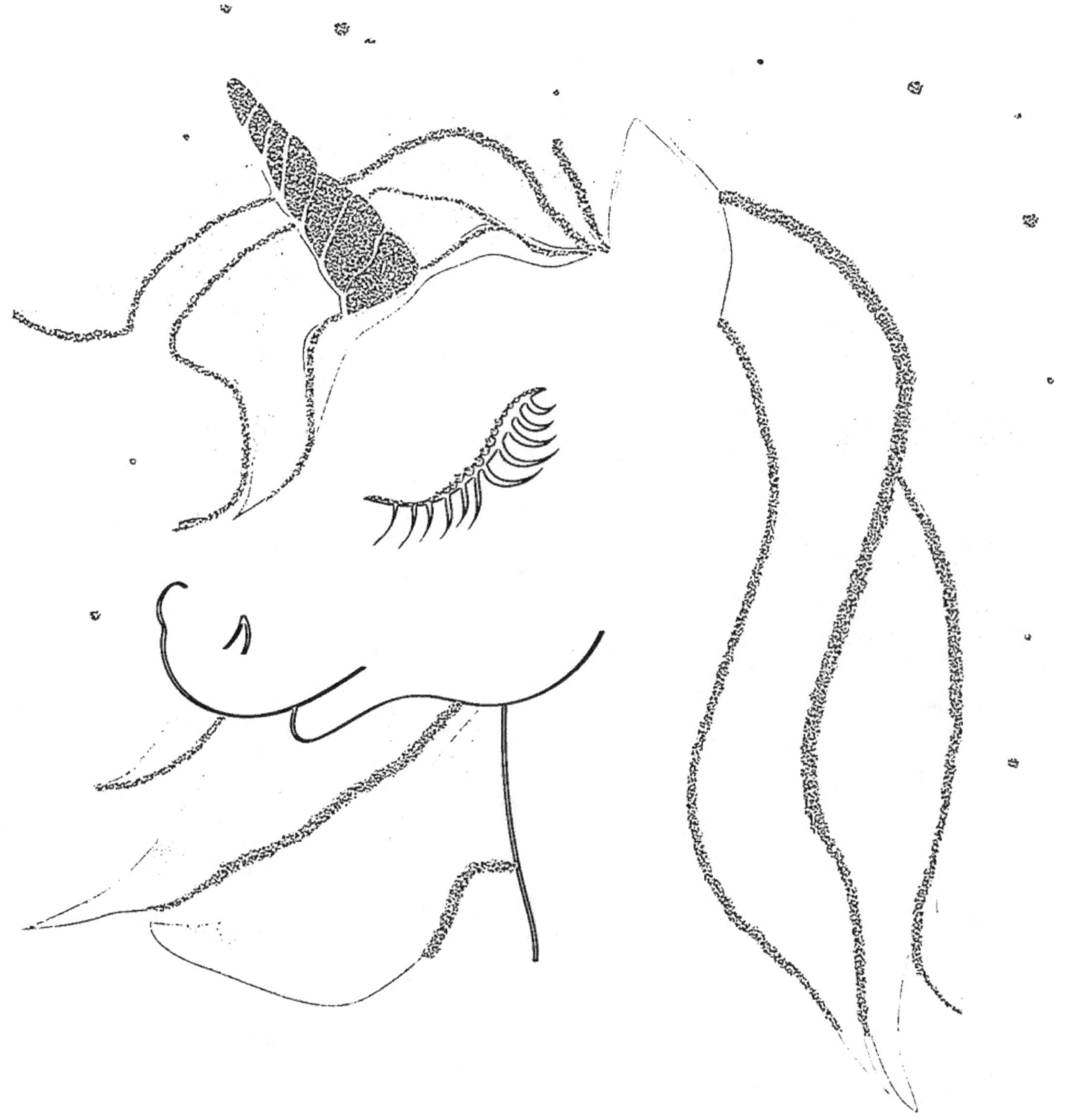